The Teen's Book of Shadows

Star Signs, Spells,
Potions, and Powers

About the Author

PATRICIA TELESCO (New York) has been a part of the Neo-Pagan community for over 30 years. During that time, she penned many memorable titles, including *A Victorian Grimoire, A Floral Grimoire, Herbal Arts, Money Magic,* and *Gardening with the Goddess.*

During her speaking engagements across the U.S., Trish met many wise people working behind the scenes who blessed her with down-toearth perspectives for going forward with books and life.

The Teen's Book of Shadows

Star Signs, Spells, Potions, and Powers

Patricia Telesco

Chicago, IL

The Teen's Book of Shadows: Star Signs, Spells, Potions, and Powers © 2025 by Patricia Telesco. All rights reserved. No part of this book may be reproduced in any manner whatsoever without written permission from Crossed Crow Books, except in the case of brief quotations embodied in critical articles and reviews.

Paperback ISBN: 978-1-964537-14-6
Library of Congress Control Number on file.

Disclaimer: Crossed Crow Books, LLC does not participate in, endorse, or have any authority or responsibility concerning private business transactions between our authors and the public. Any internet references contained in this work were found to be valid during the time of publication, however, the publisher cannot guarantee that a specific reference will continue to be maintained. This book's material is not intended to diagnose, treat, cure, or prevent any disease, disorder, ailment, or any physical or psychological condition. The author, publisher, and its associates shall not be held liable for the reader's choices when approaching this book's material. The views and opinions expressed within this book are those of the author alone and do not necessarily reflect the views and opinions of the publisher.

Published by:
Crossed Crow Books, LLC
518 Davis St, Suite 205
Evanston, IL 60201
www.crossedcrowbooks.com

Printed in the United States of America.
IBI

Other Books from Patricia Telesco

Mastering Candle Magic:
A Handbook of Advanced Spells & Charms

Spinning Spells, Weaving Wonders:
Modern Magic for Everyday Life

The Herbal Arts: A Handbook of Plant Magic,
Folklore, Recipes, Spells, & Charms

A Witch's Book of Wisdom:

A Witch's Book of Ceremonies and Rituals

Gardening with the Goddess:
A Witch's Guide to Creating Magical Gardens

Money Magic:
A Handbook of Spells and Charms for Prosperity

Your Book of Shadows:
How to Write Your Own Magical Spells

Advanced Witchcraft:
Exploring Deeper Levels of Masterful Magic

For our young adults:

Walk the path of beauty with courage, honor, and compassion.

Table of Contents

PREFACE
i

CHAPTER ONE:
Coming Home to Magic
1

CHAPTER TWO:
Bell, Book, and Candle:
Making Your Own Book of Shadows
31

CHAPTER THREE:
Getting Started
59

CHAPTER FOUR:
Come Sit for a Spell:
Locker Charms and Backpack Blessings
87

CHAPTER FIVE:
Star Signs: Applied Astrology
123

CHAPTER SIX:
Future-telling: Divination Made Easy
155

CHAPTER SEVEN:
Bedroom Feng Shui
191

CHAPTER EIGHT:
Rituals Around the Wheel
217

FINAL WORDS
249

Preface

You see a video on social media of a witch chanting over candles and going over the uses of different herbs. You may have even stumbled upon a podcast interview with an established witch and wondered, what gives? These people don't sound anything like what you've seen in movies. In fact, they sound like they might live next door. In fact, they likely do!

You're not alone. Around the world, there are thousands of young adults discovering that witchcraft is nothing like what they grew up watching. There's no eye of newt, no toads, and absolutely no instant hair color changes (except from a bottle). There's also no demon-chasing and no broom-flying, no matter how much we might wish to get out of traffic jams. In short, witches generally get a bad rap even when their practices and beliefs are discovered to be completely different from what previous portraits imply.

I'll wait until later to explain why and how all these misconceptions about the Craft and witchery began. What's most important at this point is knowing that the Craft can represent a positive and life-affirming way of living. It can also promote individuality, creativity, and personal empowerment.

See, witchcraft is alive and exciting. It is cutting-edge spirituality forged with personal vision. It's no wonder why many find it appealing. Rather than having a practice or a faith that's as dry and bland as three-day-old toast, this is as refreshing and interesting as a spring day's bike ride, hike, or hang-gliding adventure.

Now, having said that, you should know up front that witchcraft isn't for everyone. I'm not here to bash a book, tell you what to believe, how to behave, or how to find your path. Instead, the purpose of *The Teen's Book of Shadows* is to provide realistic information about the practice of witchcraft for those who are sincerely interested in learning more. In the pages of this book, you'll find practical information on everything from talking to your parents about witchcraft to casting your first spell and writing your first ritual.

Some of you might be sitting there thinking: "Who, me? I can't cast a spell, let alone write a ritual. I have no training." There's nothing to stress over. For one thing, I'll never ask you to try something that doesn't feel right or that has aspects with which you're uncomfortable, nor should you ever take a faster spiritual pace than the one your heart recognizes as right for you. If anyone ever pressures you about these things—run away quickly. It's one of the big signs of a manipulative ego out of control. You have enough to manage without adding the witchcraft equivalent of a drama king or queen to the list. Always remember this is your life, not mine or anyone else's. Right here and right now, claim it and start trusting yourself to know what's good for you.

Once you've done that, you can read this (or any) book with a more critical eye. I truly believe that anything that's truthful for your life will come back to you again and again through unrelated sources. It will find you later if it's meant to be. There is no reason to hurry your choice of spiritual paths, nor is there any immediate need to wholly transform your ways of thinking and being. Change is good, but slow and steady change is more lasting! Take the best of what you find here—the things that are really helpful and meaningful to you—and put them to use.

So, what exactly will you find here? First, we'll look at the variety of Neo-Pagan traditions available to you, and what Neo-Wicca offers specifically. More importantly, we'll consider how to best handle your decision to practice the Craft in terms of getting your family's permission and support (if possible). And if that's not possible, there are alternatives so don't despair.

Once you overcome those hurdles, *The Teen's Book of Shadows* will go on to tell you how to make your own Book of Shadows and what kinds of things to put in it. From locker charms and backpack blessings to star signs and spellcraft, you'll find a ton of ideas, information, and hands-on examples that are perfect for your book or for adapting and applying in your personal practices. Better still, you'll find these materials are very budget friendly. You won't find anything in here that's weird or requires odd ingredients. In fact, almost all the items for activities are typically found in and around your home already!

So, rather than talk about it more, let's just do it! Turn the page, get comfortable, and welcome to my world!

Chapter 1

Coming Home to Magic

Almost everyone I know who practices magic did not grow up in a Neo-Pagan home. Their families were Lutheran, Catholic, Jewish, agnostic, or any number of other faiths and non-faiths. Take me, for example. My folks were Lutheran. Most of my friends were Catholic. By the time I got to high school, I was interested in the Assemblies of God church, and then, finally, I found my way to the Craft, where I have remained for nearly forty years.

Despite the differing backgrounds and experiences, nearly all witches I've met describe the discovery of witchcraft as a "coming home" experience. It seems as if the basic ideas and ideals of this path were something developed on an individualistic level, long before they even knew other people felt similarly. You may find you feel the same way as you read about magic and witchcraft—like it feels very familiar and sounds like what's been in your heart, even when you had no words to describe what you felt.

This awareness, unfortunately, doesn't help you answer all the nagging questions about witchcraft and magic. Nor does it help people in your age group explain this information to family and friends. That's where this chapter begins.

Paganism and Your Parents

Before sharing anything else with you, it's very important that you take the time, right now, to figure out who your safe confidants are. Depending on your background and a multitude of other factors, your parents may or may not be safe people to discuss your interest in alternative faiths with. It's unfortunate, and in an ideal world you'd be able to talk to them about anything, but the sad truth is that's not always the case. So, if your parents or guardians aren't going to be receptive to the ideas, talk to your aunts and uncles, cousins, grandparents, family friends, or other trusted adults in your life. You may not feel wholly comfortable in this, but it's absolutely vital in maintaining good relationships, and they may be able to help you find the best way to talk to your parents. See, coming to adults honestly and openly shows thoughtfulness, consideration, maturity, and a sense of responsibility.

I realize this isn't the way you probably expected this book to begin, so let me explain. My sixteen-year-old son has read parts of this book, and he's helped me see things from two viewpoints— that of an average teenager and my own. From his perspective, he wants me to respect his opinions and allow him to make his own choices. He wants my trust, and he wants me to treat him like an adult member of this family. His spiritual choice (presently) is to remain agnostic. Considering our family has a very eclectic blend of spiritualities, that works just fine. The fact that he comes to me, asks questions, and thinks about the answers means a great deal to me. This is the way I would want anyone else to treat my son when it comes to anything important and life-changing. From my perspective, trust is something one earns, and I know that everyone makes mistakes sometimes based on peer pressure, or for any number of other reasons.

That's why I'm saying that it's much better just to get things out in the open. If you feel you cannot do this—you may be better off stopping right here, putting the book down, and forgetting about witchcraft for a while. It will still be there for you if it's meant to be. Re-approach the idea when you can be open and honest about it, even if that means waiting until you've moved out.

Why would I tell you to wait? For one thing, you need to remember that the words "witchcraft" and "magic" make a lot of people antsy, if not downright fearful. Most parents have a limited amount of knowledge about what those words really mean outside of what they've heard in church or on TV. Their uncertain reaction is normal, but you have another disadvantage due to your age. Adults don't always respect a teen's ideas or opinions because we feel you might not be seeing the whole picture and you don't have the advantage of extra years of life experiences to guide your choices. That doesn't mean you're necessarily going to make a "wrong" decision, but it's our spiritual job and ethical duty as parents and concerned adults to advise you to the best of our ability.

As a minor living at home, there are some rules to follow and lines of communication to carefully preserve. Family is very important, and while you might not always agree with your folks, and they may not always approve of all you do, that bond is lifelong. I would much rather see you proceed slowly or wait until you're an adult than permanently put a barrier between you and any member of that familial unit. If you take nothing else away from this book, please treasure this one lesson: faith and a positive spiritual focus should draw people together, not push them apart.

Witchcraft doesn't allow us to neatly keep our family life separate from our magical life. In fact, one of the main goals of magical living is to bring that special energy into every moment of every day and allow its ideals into all our relationships. That's kind of hard to do if you can't be open and honest.

Let's start, however, with those of you who feel you can go to your parents to talk about this choice. The next question is where to begin. Well, first consider with what circumstances you're dealing. Are your parents practicing a particular faith, and if so, how devoutly? Do they have any particular beliefs or practices to which you already relate or that seem close to something you've noticed in the Craft? If so, you've got a good starting point. Always stress what's alike versus what's different (trust me, you'll have plenty of time discussing differences later).

If there isn't a mutual ground on which to start things off, then you need to be prepared with the answers to the questions most parents have. This chapter helps you with that by sharing the different jargon used in the Craft: what words mean, how they're used, and, of course, quite simply, what it is that witches do and believe. Have this information firmly in hand when you talk to your parents. You may also want to get a copy of another beginner's witchcraft book. I like Scott Cunningham's *The Truth About Witchcraft Today,* which is old (so take its information with a grain of salt) but very straightforward and down-to-earth. These two things together will help your family understand what modern magic is all about and hopefully undo some of the preconceived notions and concerns that may very well stand between you and your practice.

Mind you, bringing up your new choice isn't the best conversation to just spring on people at dinner, or to address when things are already stressed at home. Wait until there's a calm moment—one where you'll have the least interruptions and ask for a meeting. Bring everything

Coming Home to Magic 5

with you, including your convictions, and be ready to answer your family's questions in a simple, respectful way. Remember, they may have odd ideas about the Craft being evil or some kind of cult, and you have to show them the positive influence metaphysical ideals can have on your life.

While I will be covering some of these points in more detail throughout this chapter, here are just a few good things to bring up in your conversation:

- Neo-Wicca, Neo-Paganism, and many forms of witchcraft are predominantly earth-based traditions, predominantly focused on respecting the Earth and its creatures.
- The importance of honor, respect, gratitude, and tolerance in Neo-Wiccan ideology.
- Spiritual education is important to the Neo-Wiccan belief system. The Craft is not a shake-and-bake religion—it's one that uses the mind that God/dess gave us to learn and grow.
- This path provides a sense of self-confidence and improved control over one's life.
- Taking personal responsibility for your actions, inactions, and choices are stressed. In all Neo-Pagan traditions, your life is what you make of it, and when you mess up—you clean up!
- The fact that attention is given to thinking before one acts (i.e., balancing our hearts and heads, and using the mind we've got for sound reasoning, even in matters of faith—or, perhaps more aptly, especially in matters of faith!).
- The fact that Neo-Wicca teaches respect toward each person's choice of faith (including that of your parents). Neo-Wicca stresses a non-sexist approach toward

people and Deity. No matter your gender, when practicing Neo-Wicca, you're still a witch. One is not greater or better than the other—just different, and both genders are respected for what they bring to life and magic.

Just as a side note, this is not the time to push boundaries that will put your parents on edge. You want to be listened to and not add fuel to what could be a rather heated discussion. So, show up to the conversation in a way that will promote respect on both sides. Take a deep breath, wear something comfortable that helps you feel empowered, and be willing to listen as well as speak.

Now, I know some of you are already thinking, "what if all this doesn't work? What if they object to my studies and interest, or want to limit me in some way?" First, try negotiating. For example, if your parents are worried about you burning candles and incense in your room because it's a fire risk, try LED candles and room sprays instead. That way you honor the house rules, show you can be responsible with their request, and still accomplish your goals.

Alternatively, if their objection is more deep-seated, perhaps you can work out a time or work-share trade, like attending special family functions (that you would otherwise avoid) with them or adding a new chore into your household routine. In return, ask that they allow you a specific amount of time to devote to your spiritual interests.

If both these approaches fail, my best advice is to honor your parents' wishes. You can certainly re-approach them in six or twelve months and try again (sometimes persistence pays off because it shows your interest wasn't short-lived or a "fad"). You can also still read about witchcraft at the library or talk about it with friends. But ultimately, respecting your parents' decisions in and around your home is the right thing to do, including from a magical perspective.

Think of it this way—we talk about tolerance, love, and trust as keynotes to our beliefs. If you cannot give those things to people who provide for and nurture you, how can you possibly hope to give it to anyone else? (In the case where your parents aren't safe allies or, worst case scenario, actively put you in harm's way, I'm sorry. Keep "tolerance" in the forefront here.) Also, anything that you care deeply about will still be part of your heart and mind when you turn eighteen.

Being a witch is more about who you are inside and how you let that affect the way you live your life than it is about all the bells and whistles, like spells. You can portray your ideals and be the magic, without waving it in people's faces and making them uncomfortable. Living and thinking globally also includes your own home. Begin there, gently, and sensitively, and you're well on your way to establishing a strong spiritual path that will not lead you astray.

Myth, Adventures, and Lingering Lore

There is a lot of folklore and superstition still lingering about Neo-Wicca and witches. Since these are among the first things anyone jokes or asks about, let's undo some of them right away. For example, real witches do not ride on brooms. That story originated from old Pagan crop rites where people would jump up and down upon brooms. The idea was that they were showing the crops how to grow toward the sky with their leaping.

Another very common myth is the image of witches as old hags complete with pointy hats. This particular depiction comes in part from the elderly crone aspect of the Goddess who can be a little frightening when She reminds us of our mortality. Another part was the historical old woman in the village who was seen as a nuisance and therefore branded as a witch. The other part was a simple misrepresentation intended to frighten people away from folk magic and into the churches. And for a while, it worked quite well.

Worse still, not only did the ancients think that witches lacked fashion sense, but we also were given all manner of ugly birthmarks that "revealed" our true calling. From an armpit birthmark to warts on our noses, the witch became quite a frightful sight. Beyond the church feeding this type of image to a mostly illiterate and naive public, the public was also honestly afraid sometimes. Life was harsh and held few answers. Folks wanted something to give them the sense that they could control unseen powers and influences somehow. So, making up stories of how to recognize a witch made perfect sense. After all, forewarned is forearmed!

Other signs that ancient people looked for to determine whether a person was a witch included:

- Having squinty or crossed eyes.
- Having eyebrows that met over the nose.
- Possessing a broom, a cauldron, or anything else someone considered a "witchy" tool (my kitchen is dangerous!).
- Having gray hair, living alone, and owning many different animals.

Of course, these things seem like broad brushing to the modern eye, and they are all certainly generalizations that were based on superficial externals. But even today, people jump on the condemnation bandwagon based on how someone looks, so we can't judge our ancestors too harshly. Nonetheless, one or more of these things got a fair number of people in serious trouble during the witch-hunts, sometimes even leading to death.

Older books that describe witches in this drab and demeaning manner also oddly praise their powers. We read of witches flying, casting spells, raising spirits, divining the future, turning invisible, animating objects, raising the wind, and changing into animals. All in all, I can live with that kind of reputation, but the portrait still isn't wholly accurate. I already explained the flying aspect, and modern witches still use spells, divinations, and weather magic. However, most leave the concept of raising spirits to High (or Ritual) Magicians, animating objects seems to have all but disappeared (but for theories), and shapeshifting is of interest mostly among ecstatic witches.

This brief overview shows how Neo-Wicca has grown and changed with time. The flexibility and forward-looking aspect of this belief system is among its greatest attributes. Rather than stagnate in old, outworn beliefs and practices, Neo-Wiccans re-create themselves with the deftness of a chameleon. We realize that the world around us transforms quickly, and if we don't keep up and allow our spiritual path to reflect new knowledge and social consciousness, the magic will die.

Although this has been a very brief overview of the old beliefs about witches, I still think it's important that you have it in mind, along with good explanations, just in case! You never know what kind of superstitions people have until you launch into a subject like magic with them. And, by the way, if any of the answers you need are not here, and you're not certain, it's really okay to tell people, "I don't know." After that response, do a little research and ask some practitioners about the issue you were unsure about. Then, return to the person who posed the question with accurate information. This is much better than making up an answer. While it may save face momentarily, it usually comes back to bite you on the butt.

Neo-Wiccans, Witches, and Magic

Okay, now we need to back up and take a look at Neo-Wicca, witchcraft, and metaphysics in general. Your parents will probably wonder what Neo-Wiccans do, if Neo-Wiccans and witches are the same thing, and why there seems to be so much fuss about this magic stuff. This section represents a very brief overview of a complex and varied system in the hopes of undoing some stereotypes and providing a glimpse into the real world of modern magic as opposed to what your parents may have seen on TV or heard in church.

To begin, let's define terms. Magic is the willful gathering and redirecting of energy for a specific purpose. Some people choose to spell it with a "k" at the end to differentiate it from stage magic and sleight-of-hand. There are many ways that magical practitioners accomplish this gathering and redirecting. We might cast a spell, enact a ritual, create a charm, offer up prayers, or try focused meditations (none of which evoke flashing lights or demonic stalkers).

A witch is someone who uses magic as a tool to effect change, but that's only one part of a much bigger picture. Neo-Wicca is a blending of religion, philosophy, and methodology to create a way of life that's positive and affirming. It is certainly not all about casting spells and working rituals. In fact, I can count on the fingers of one hand the number of spells I've done in the last few months.

Why so few? Because witches tend to be self-sufficient, meaning if we can do it ourselves mundanely, we do! Magic is not meant to be a crutch. It's a tool—nothing more, nothing less.

God?

Some witches are monotheistic, believing in a Sacred Parent that is both male and female, both and neither. The monotheistic witch may or may not consider this Being interactive. Some feel the Divine can, and does, work as a co-creator with us, while others see this Power as an inception point (the spark behind the big bang) and nothing more. The rest of the energy for their magic comes from the life force all around us—in nature, the earth, the stars, etc.

Other witches are polytheistic. They believe in a variety of gods and goddesses who help guide and direct our magic and to whom we can turn for insights and aid in daily living. Additionally, most witches have a very strong connection to nature, seeing it as a reflection of the Divine, and as a key to understanding some of the universe's mysteries.

How does this relate to the mainstream ideas of God? That depends on how you view the universe. I will share with you how I explained it to my folks some thirty-eight years ago, and maybe that will help. Basically, I told them that I thought of the Divine like a huge, multi-faceted crystal. What each person perceives in that crystal depends on where they stand and to what facet they look. With the human mind having mortal limitations, there's only so much we can understand of anything so huge. So, we put God in a box—with a name like YHWH, Diana, Zeus, and so forth. Of course, since we consider ourselves children of this being, He or She also receives attributes, characteristics, and an image that somehow reflects part of humanity. In other words, we create God/dess in our own image in an attempt to explain the seemingly inexplicable.

I went on to share that I felt that this Divine crystal shattered at the beginning of time. One small shard of it landed within each human soul. That's why we have this inner desire to return to God/dess, and why we seek out other spiritually minded people. We're trying to put our puzzle back together the right way. If this description somehow helps you, great! If not, you'll have to find your own words to describe how you see God and why.

The Pentagram

One of the best symbols that reflects witchcraft ideals, and the most often misunderstood one, is the pentagram. The five points on the pentagram represent the four elements (Earth, Air, Fire, and Water) and the fifth element of Spirit. All of these energies are harmoniously placed within a circle—an emblem of cycles, time, sacred space, and the source of all things. This is the perfect representation of everything that Neo-Wiccans hope to obtain: a sense of self in the greater scheme of things, an awareness of others and the earth, and welcoming sacred energies into our lives on a daily basis. Does this all happen overnight? Heavens, no! Most practitioners will tell you that the more they study and learn, the more they realize how little they actually know.

This symbolic value differs dramatically from an upside-down pentacle often displayed in movies as a sign of evil. Just as an upside-down cross is sacrilegious, an upside-down pentacle is very offensive to a Neo-Wiccan. Our belief system does not include "Satan" in the Christian sense, and most witches strive to protect life and goodness, not undermine it.

Warlock, Neo-Wiccan, Witch? Who Is Who?

First, as I mentioned before, men who practice witchcraft are generally called witches and not warlocks. The word warlock has very negative connotations, having originated in the 1400s as a term meaning "oath breaker." So, I wouldn't call a male witch a "warlock" unless they have expressed a preference for that term.

What of the word "witch" itself? Well, it seems to have come from an Anglo-Saxon term *wicce* that means "a practitioner of sorcery." Until the Crusades, this term was applied to men and women equally and didn't carry a lot of negative overtones. Typically, these people learned their art from a family member or village elder. They practiced quietly, often as part of a village structure, using their skills to aid the sick, improve crop growth, and provide sound advice for commoners and kings alike. Historically, witches and diviners were among the first psychologists and guidance counselors, knowing that a kind gesture could often do more good than a potion or charm.

Obviously, things have changed with time. As I mentioned earlier, witches pride themselves on adapting their arts and perspectives to the changes in science and the earth. Witches also live everywhere (there's usually more than one of us in any town or city) and some are more active in our communities than others. Nonetheless, many things remain the same. We still use herbal formulas, we still cast spells, and we still end up dispensing advice. It's part of our tradition, and it's all good!

So, what is it exactly that separates a witch from someone who is Neo-Wiccan? Basically, Wicca is an initiatory religion (meaning you need to be trained and initiated by someone already in it), a philosophy, and a system of ethics. Neo-Wicca is a more open non-initiatory practice and religion that is made up of the open/public parts of Wicca, as well as other teachings that predominantly came about in the eighties and nineties. Not all witches are Neo-Wiccan because not all choose to follow Neo-Wiccan rules or ideals in their practices. On the other hand, you'd be hard pressed to find a Neo-Wiccan who is not a witch!

Rules of Neo-Wicca

Since we're on the topic, what are the "rules" of Neo-Wicca? The most common is called the Threefold Law, and it states that whatever you send out comes back to you three times. Akin to the Christian ideal of "do unto others," the Threefold Law makes a great argument for being the proverbial "good witch" all the time! I mean, who of us wants bad stuff coming back three times?

The other most common rule boils down to "harm none," including yourself. This rule is harder than it might seem to follow. Harming none means we can't go around manipulating people—making them fall in love with us, for example. It also means taking care of our planet, our families, and ourselves in a sensible way. The planet in particular lays heavy on our hearts right now because it is among our greatest teachers and a source of wholeness, but humankind has abused its gifts very badly. Similarly, a lot of people really struggle with self-confidence and self-image. The rule of harm none applies to your outlooks and attitudes, too. The power of positive thinking shouldn't be overlooked as being cliché.

Which brings me to another guideline in Neo-Wicca—that of responsibility (this is a point most parents really like). Neo-Wiccans feel that we are wholly responsible for the energy we send out and everything that energy affects in the web of life (even those things we didn't think about or couldn't possibly predict). Again, this is a good cause for really thinking over one's motivations and goals before casting any spells or even before getting involved in Neo-Wicca at all. This isn't a game or a power trip—it's not a way to mess with people, and it shouldn't be treated like that, either.

I always tell my students that if they're not willing to work for something on a mundane level, don't bother working magic for it either. This is part of our "job" as witches. Since each person in our belief system becomes their own Priest or Priestess, and since we consider ourselves co-creators, this makes perfect sense. The "do as I say, not as I do" school of thought just doesn't cut it here. Magic is at least 80% hard work. Anyone who tells you otherwise isn't, in my opinion, being honest or ethical.

Fundamentalist Neo-Wiccans?

Another key word in Neo-Wicca is *tolerance*. Witches do not try to convert anyone. If someone comes to us with honest questions, that's great. We will answer those questions and provide as much information as possible, but we will not try to dissuade them from a currently practiced faith. In my case, I'll check to make sure that the person asking me is eighteen or older, and if not, I send them right back to their parents. Why? Because this illustrates honor and respect. Witches see each person's spiritual vision as one road among many, all of which lead to the same place—enlightenment.

This is a very strong point to share with your family because it shows that you don't intend to take a Book of Shadows out to street corners and start calling on the God/dess publicly! It also lets them know that their beliefs are just as important and valid as yours. Quite honestly, aside from those closest to you, no one needs to know about your faith—it is a private matter and up to you to decide with whom you share it.

Witchcraft Denominations?

As in Christianity, there are also a lot of "sects" or "schools" of magic, each of which has a specific flavor and focus. There are hereditary witches who learn their methods from family tradition, but they are fairly rare simply because up until recently, it hasn't been overly safe to be a witch publicly or privately (at some points in history it could get you killed).

For those who do not have an enchanted family tree, other options exist. Some might choose to look to Celtic traditions, others to Egyptian, others to Dianic (a feminist focus), and others still to folk traditions, just to name a few. There are a lot of underlying similarities between each of these, but the rituals, words, and techniques will vary among schools of thought, and among each group practicing them.

Let's take Ceremonial Magic, another form of High Magic, as an example. Ceremonial Magic is considered an occult path, but it doesn't necessarily operate within Neo-Pagan constructs. It also tends to be much more detailed and precise in its methods than some other approaches. Most who practice Ceremonial Magic consider themselves magicians or sorcerers, but not all consider themselves witches or pagans. Similarly, Druids are often grouped under Neo-Pagan traditions, but they don't consider themselves witches (although some witches adopt a Druidic theme in their work).

All of this can become very confusing. How do you know which witch is which? Your best bet is to just ask but be prepared for some more confusing answers. If you were to ask ten witches to define their spiritual path, you'd get ten different answers, even if those ten witches were practicing the same school of magic! This happens because we stress personal vision in exploring witchcraft, which is already complex and filled with symbols and ideas that can be interpreted differently depending on the cultural influences and magical traditions involved. Effectively, there could be as many denominations of witches as there are practitioners.

This diversity is both good and bad. It's going to make it hard for you to pinpoint exactly what a witch does and believes to your family. So rather than going for the big picture, stick to what you know—namely what you feel witchcraft offers you as an individual and what parts of witchcraft appeal to you (and why). Don't make this whole discussion more complex than it needs to be. It's enough to know that there are a lot of positive approaches to magic, and among them you've found one that works for you! If they want more information on the many forms of witchery, there are many good books available and any witchcraft shop owner would be happy to point them in the right direction.

And What of Magic?

Magic is but one part of Neo-Wicca, but it is an important part. In looking at history, we find that magic was practiced in all ancient civilizations in one form or another. Modern practitioners have "borrowed" from the past, keeping the best ideas and adapting the rest so they reflect our times. For example, while many ancient societies offered animals on the altars to gods and goddesses, Neo-Wiccans do not do this. The call to heal our planet and the awareness that such sacrifices are not necessary both contribute to the change that occurred.

So, while some of the ideas, methods, and practices of the modern magical movement are very old, realistically, Neo-Wicca is a young religion just making real public headway (having seen exponential growth starting around the 1970s). Surveys indicate that Neo-Wicca is among the fastest-growing religions in the U.S. and Canada today. These numbers include groups and solitary practitioners. Wicca is even officially recognized by the U.S. military and written up in every chaplain's handbook (another good point to share with your family).

Covens and Circles: Neo-Wiccan Collectives and Activities

Speaking of groups, a Neo-Wiccan group is often called a coven, and our gatherings are often called circles (with other names suited to the occasion). Samples of magical circles have been seen in the media, but these are very limited. Do not anticipate that an actual Neo-Wiccan ritual will be anything like that, or you'll be disappointed. Magic is serious business, and when a group gathers together to raise energy, they should take that task seriously. This doesn't mean not having any fun, nor does it mean dressing in sackcloth and ashes, but it does mean maintaining a certain level of respect.

In order for a coven to function well, each person in the circle is depended upon for their input. Sometimes a person might have an active role in the magic (like lighting a candle or reciting a verse), and other times their only role is to focus energy toward its goal—but both are necessary and important. This is why you see witches meeting in circles, which represent equality and the never-ending wheel of time and life!

What exactly happens in a circle? A lot of things. Sometimes we gather to commemorate the time of year (like the solstices and equinoxes). Sometimes we gather to try to meet a need in our community. Other times still we gather just to celebrate our magic and our friendship. A strong bond exists in magical groups, and the ties often run very deep.

Having said that, it's good to know that about 70% of the witchcraft community practices their art alone as solitaries. Some do this to avoid group politics. Others prefer to carve out a path that's wholly personalized (and therefore individually more meaningful). Others still go this route for lack of any other choice (perhaps they're traveling abroad or live in the Bible Belt). So, if the idea of meeting with a group of witches makes your family uneasy, you may want to offer solitary practice as an alternative or invite your family to an open circle to meet the rest of the group.

At the beginning of my practice, I dove in alone. And while there were times that being solitary got difficult (you don't have anyone to bounce ideas off of), it really taught me to trust myself. Better still, because I wasn't constrained to one particular magical flavor, I discovered a lot of global methods that I use to this day. All in all, it's been a very satisfying and exciting way to live, but only you can decide whether you prefer working solo or with a group.

Thirteen Common Questions about Magic and Witchcraft

Even with the growing popularity of Neo-Pagan belief systems, there are still some age-old questions people ask repeatedly about this lifestyle. More than likely, at least four of these questions will come from your family and friends. So, in the spirit of "forewarned is forearmed," here they are (in no particular order), along with some answers to help get you off on the right foot.

Question: *Are witches evil? (Do they worship Satan or another malevolent figurehead?)*
Answer: There are good witches and bad witches, just like there are good Christians and bad Christians. What constitutes "good" or "bad" here is typically motivations, actions, and other behaviors that outweigh any amount of lip service. Having said that, witches as a whole have gotten a bad rap for thousands of years, partially because they worship a being that isn't part of the "mainstream" belief system.

To understand this, realize that modern witchcraft most likely developed out of paganism, Hebrew mysticism, and Greek and Roman beliefs (among other influences). When churches began to object to those influences, the portrait of a witch was purposefully demonized, becoming the ugly old hag meant to scare people away. The Devil with his horns was also a clever adaptation of popular horned nature gods.

This sort of negative characterization of an old religion by a new one certainly wasn't unique. It's been done again and again throughout history, but because of people's superstitious nature, the lack of literacy, and overall fear of the church's power, the image took firm hold in some quarters. So, while the image remained, the reality of what witches are and what they believe went mostly unknown until the last century.

Question: *Can a person be both a Christian and a witch?*
Answer: Since there are various forms of mysticism in Christianity (for example, Knights Templar) and in Jewish tradition (such as Cabalists), there is no reason not to believe the basic methods of witchcraft, specifically magic, could not be utilized by someone on a Christian path, or that of any other religion for that matter. Things like meditation and prayer are already part of all these belief systems, and individuals are free to blend compatible ideals and techniques together so one does not conflict with or overshadow the other.

Question: *If witchcraft can be blended with any faith, and there are many types of witches, how do we know who to turn to for accurate information? Can there be such a thing as "accurate information" in a vision-driven belief system?*
Answer: Yes, you can get accurate information, and the best bet is by word of mouth. Go to several individuals from the specific path that you have questions about and see who they recommend (or what books and websites). While you're still likely to get some differing data, look to the continuity—the phrases or concepts that repeat themselves in three different (unrelated) sources. Those are the things to which to pay close attention.

Question: *How many people currently practice some form of Neo-Paganism?*
Answer: Since witches and Neo-Pagans don't have churches per se, and some feel the need to keep their beliefs

anonymous, getting numbers is difficult. I can, however, use some of the most popular sites on the web as a gauge. If we consider that the Witches' Voice (also known as Witchvox) was getting hits from nearly 400,000 unique users monthly in summer 2002 (and that number increased exponentially every month), we can safely assume the actual numbers of people practicing are much higher. The rise of social media helped those numbers: in winter 2024, twenty-two years later, there were *5 million* videos tagged with "witch" on TikTok. More interesting still is the wide variety of people we find in this community. Young and old, scientist and artist, construction worker and office worker—Neo-Pagans come from every walk of life, and only a handful of them grew up in Neo-Pagan homes.

Question: *Is there one predominant form of witchcraft?*
Answer: If I had to pinpoint one common denominator in Neo-Paganism, it would be the practice of the cunning arts (folk magic). These simple, hearth-and-home approaches to magic are represented in nearly every metaphysical path I've come across. While the words and actions may vary slightly, the core of these approaches—coming out of daily needs, symbols, and experiences—is the same.

Folk magic came out of the practices of common people who did not have superstores or computers. These people creatively turned to the items that were on hand, and that made sense to their goals. The reason this path has remained so strong is that it's incredibly adaptable, and works marvelously in our frequently time-challenged, budget-oriented world.

Question: *Why don't witches have churches or something similar?*

Answer: There are a variety of reasons. Someone once said, "the groves were the gods' first temples." Combine this sentiment with the Pagan love for nature and you begin to understand why walls wouldn't be very important. When you see the God/dess as within and without all things, a specific location even seems a little silly but for convenience of assembly.

Don't stop there, however. Add to this foundation the idea that walls imply exclusivity rather than the inclusiveness implied by the circle. We do not wish to keep people out. Even more important, since our community is stretched across the world, and highly diversified, where exactly might one put a "church"?

Most witches believe that sacred space is truly a matter of attitude. It can be wherever you are, simply by shifting your awareness. That's not to say some efforts aren't underway to have tracts of land dedicated to our faith. Numerous groups around the US have bought acreage in order to have a permanent spot on which to hold gatherings and festivals. These spaces are usually built within the ideals of particular traditions but are generally open to all in the spirit of sharing our common bonds and celebrating diversity.

Question: *So how does someone who's interested in the Craft find other Neo-Pagans?*
Answer: Since Neo-Wicca and other Neo-Pagan traditions haven't been mainstream until recently, people developed strong networking ties. As one met another, they exchanged addresses, shared information, and created an infrastructure based on good communication. We utilize every means that can potentially be utilized to keep people "in the loop" including social media, traditions, and local witchcraft stores. It can take some time to find

a person or group through this method, but thanks to the internet, it usually doesn't take too long.

Question: *Is there anything of which to be wary?*
Answer: Of course. Any time there is an emotional or spiritual upswell, keeping a healthy dose of common sense, skepticism, and objectivity in your back pocket is a good thing. With witchcraft becoming more popular, there are going to be individuals, groups, writers, teachers, and shopkeepers who get involved only to make a buck, feel powerful, or to massage their ego. Unfortunately, that's human nature.

Briefly, avoid any group or organization that makes claims of having 100% fool-proof results. There are no such guarantees in matters of faith. Second, be cautious of those asking for a lot of money for what seems to be a small item or service. Just like at the supermarket, price does not ensure quality (and I personally do not believe that spiritual pursuits should make or break anyone's budget).

Third, watch out for people who insist that you must do something against your ethics or values in order to take part in their group or activities. That's a huge warning sign that indicates this person or group has an agenda that isn't in your best interest.

Fourth, steer clear of those who promote exclusivity, or who seem to be more focused on quantity than quality. I have seen groups who are more interested in showing off their large membership as opposed to actually teaching and training that membership.

If you follow those four simple guidelines, you'll usually avoid the drama queens and kings, and other high-maintenance people.

Question: *I hear a lot about spells and rituals—what type of results do these techniques produce?*
Answer: That depends heavily on both circumstances and the practitioners. In magic, it's very important that a person understands what they are doing and why. It's also important to have a strong mental and spiritual connection to not only the process but all the symbols used in it. Without that connection, without focus, without will or faith, nothing's going to happen. To put this into context, think of all the prayers recited without thought in church—many people have no real connection to what they're saying; it's just rote, so no energy goes into it. Magic works similarly—there must be feeling and comprehension to drive manifestation.

In terms of circumstantial issues—spells or rituals that get interrupted by the phone, a neighbor visiting, or whatever—often don't work simply because the focus gets lost. So, the results from magic can be absolutely nothing to the nearly miraculous depending on these factors.

Question: *If that's true, what's with all the hocus-pocus on TV and in movies?*
Answer: Let's face it—real modern magic isn't that exciting to watch. There are no flashing lights, no instant hair color changes, no floating or flying, and no frogs! TV and movies are looking for audiences, and flashy effects mean big bucks.

I have no issue with that. In fact, I enjoy those flights of fancy so long as people don't think they fairly or reliably represent our community.

News reporting agencies are another story altogether. Lately, there have been at least three stories that implied

Santeria (an Afro-Cuban folk practice and religion) or witchcraft was to blame for very messy animal sacrifices that were stumbled upon after the fact. I know enough about both these systems to immediately recognize all three of these circumstances as having nothing to do with either Santeríans or Neo-Wiccans—but it's sensational, so the agencies print it anyway. Thankfully, more Neo-Pagans are watch-dogging the press and providing information to law enforcement agencies so that knock-off ritual crime can be recognized for what it is: a cheap and hideous fake that should not be ascribed to our faith.

Question: *Do witches put curses on people?*
Answer: Those individuals practicing a positive spiritual path are loath to consider such a dramatic invasion of someone else's life and free will as this. Nonetheless, I'd be lying if I told you it never happened. Neo-Pagans are just like everyone else—sometimes they get pressed to the wall and feel the need to fight back.

Question: *How do witches and Neo-Pagans feel about science and technology, since so much in these fields seems to be completely contrary to magic?*
Answer: Yesterday's "magic" is today's science and technology. Even one hundred years ago, the concept of flying beyond earth's atmosphere was nothing more than a fantasy. The first forms of chemistry were based on alchemy (a mystical and metaphysical art/science). So, Neo-Pagans see clearly that many times the vision of "magic" drives manifestation in the real world. We feel that the magic we use today can have some type of expression in the science or technology of the future.

Additionally, it's important to note that our ancestors looked to everything in and around their lives as having potential magical applications. Many modern Neo-Pagans do likewise. They employ everything from computer programming and even AI as symbols and tools to assist in spiritual goals. This is another way that our magic grows and changes to keep up with our times.

Question: *Don't all those changes make things very confusing even for people who have practiced magic for a long time?*
Answer: Not really. We believe that witchcraft needs to be forward-looking, or it will stagnate and die in mounds of dogma. As we learn more about our universe, our practices integrate that knowledge so that fact and faith can work hand in hand. Additionally, these ongoing transformations help us to focus on why we do what we do, not just how we're doing it. In other words, individual internal changes are just as important as those in our world.

Secondly, for a very long time, witchcraft was considered a woman's art that included midwifery, healing animals, and helping with wayward lovers! Since the role of women in our society has only been changing for the better for the last one hundred years, it's not surprising that witches at one time endured so much difficulty. Even today if you were to ask a dozen people if men could be witches, I bet at least nine or ten would say no. Notice how male practitioners in media often get called warlocks, wizards, and sorcerers rather than witches.

Third, it's normal for people to fear or misrepresent what they don't understand. After the witch-hunts and other similar persecution, magic went underground for a very long time to protect its people and traditions. Unfortunately, hiding solved nothing—it only made people more suspicious and fearful. So when the 1960s came around, and there seemed to be a more open-minded attitude throughout the

US, it made sense that at least a few witches would begin venturing out of the broom closet to be counted. We have done this in part to promote everyone's religious freedom, and in part so that something like the Salem witch trials never happens again.

In 1970, a whole new group of magical teachers and leaders showed their face to the world, some of whom are still writing and teaching today. Then came the New Age movement, bringing Neo-Wicca and witchcraft back into the public eye with art, music, incense, oils, candles, tools, and especially books. Some publishers offer hundreds of titles on metaphysical topics alone. And of course, the movie and television industries followed the wave by making programs that come closer to the truth of modern magic.

What all this says is that times are finally changing for witches. Many of us now gather together in public parks or on private land to celebrate our heritage openly and freely as it should be. Here we remember the past, and look to the future excitedly, wondering what other magic the world will offer us in the days and years ahead.

Is It Really for You?

Okay, now that you've had a short, informative tour of witchcraft, Neo-Wicca, and associated practices, the next obvious question becomes: is this really the right path for you? I cannot answer that, nor would I begin to try. What I can do, however, is give you some food for thought.

First, what is it specifically that you find attractive about the craft? If you're simply looking for neat robes, jewelry, and incense, just go shopping. Even if a dozen of your friends have been trying out magic, that doesn't mean it's right for you. No one should try to apply this method or its ideals just because of peer pressure—in fact, that's very un-witchy! While it's wonderful to be on the same page as friends, the decision to practice witchcraft is a very personal one that can really turn your life upside down.

Similarly, witchcraft is not about freaking out your teachers or parents. While it might seem like fun at first to toss this out as an attention-getting tool or a way of making someone mad, remember you're playing with someone else's spirituality. This is something deeply meaningful to thousands of people around the world. Don't use it to manipulate others or as a game.

On the other hand, if you're looking for a transformational way of life with a spiritual focus, you might be in the right place. In particular, you'll find that various versions of witchcraft can help you with things like improved self-confidence, focus, and regaining a sense of control with regard to your fate. Nonetheless, there is absolutely no reason to rush this choice. In fact, I advise against it. Take your time, check things out, think about it, then decide.

Should you decide this is a good place for you to be, and have gotten your parents' permission to proceed, then move ahead and finish this book! There's a lot in here for you to explore and try. I have to tell you that I envy you this process. I didn't discover the witch within until I was twenty-five. As I watch our community's young adults, I see them bearing so much wisdom, vision, and power that it's truly awe-inspiring. You can join them! Just read on!

Chapter II

Bell, Book, and Candle: Making Your Own Book of Shadows

Many witches keep what's called a Book of Shadows. Far more than simply a collection of spells, a Book of Shadows is kind of like a magical diary. It's very intimate and reflects who you are and all that you can be. It's a place where you can make notes about your spiritual path, about special rituals or herbals, about how practicing magic affects you daily, and about how you manage to blend the mundane and metaphysical together successfully into your day-to-day life.

Just like a regular diary, this book is special and very personal. Why call it a Book of Shadows? In part, this is because witches used to practice under the safety of darkness or in secret places. Thankfully, we have reclaimed the night and no longer need to go to such lengths to express our beliefs without fear. The second reason for the use of the word "shadows" is because magic is something that works between the worlds (and beyond them), in places we do not really see with our physical eyes but can sense. Somewhere, between this reality and all other possibilities, the spark of magic burns brightly until it manifests in our reality.

The purpose of this chapter is to nurture that spark by giving it a very real place to keep notes on all your magical thoughts, processes, tools, and techniques. Here, you'll find a variety of ideas on how to make your own magical diary. Just as you are a work-in-progress spiritually, this book will never really be "finished." It develops at the same pace as you do. This side-by-side development helps you see your spiritual progress in a more concrete form. That's why I recommend that you use your Book of Shadows for more than just writing—read it regularly too. Turn back to those pages regularly for insights or ideas or just to refresh your memory of a special magical moment. You will find that this tome will become a good friend, one that reveals all your potential and gifts. It's also a wonderful keepsake for the years ahead.

Where?

Before moving forward and talking about actually putting the Book of Shadows together, I'd like to offer the idea of having a special place devoted to this task. More than likely, the only private space you have is your room, so that's one possibility. Or, if the weather is good, perhaps you can work outdoors. Privacy helps with your focus which, in turn, improves the results.

Once you've found the best possible workspace, don't stop there. Think about other touches that give you a sense of doing something magical—like lighting some candles and incense. If you can't burn candles or incense in your room, perhaps you can substitute aromatherapy. Try dabbing the light bulbs or your door with a blend of lemon, cinnamon, lavender, and ginger oils (these represent spirituality, purification, harmony, and energy).

Other nice accents include decorating the area with crystals, a god or goddess statue, some fresh flowers, and, of course, anything specific to the subject matter you'll be addressing in the Book (like having herbs available when you're writing up an herbal section). Surround yourself with sights, sounds, and smells that speak of the importance of what you're doing and its meaning. Also, if you like, you can create a sacred space so that you have a quiet spiritual atmosphere in which to work.

Now, some of you may not be familiar with the idea of making your own sacred space. I promise this doesn't mean having to wear dark clothing, using Shakespearean lingo, or never cracking a smile. Quite simply, a sacred space is any area into which you've invited your vision of the Divine and the Elemental powers (Earth, Air, Fire, Water) to bless your efforts and safeguard the room. Prayers, invocations, and meditations can all be used to accomplish this.

Creating Sacred Space

For more specific details on creating formal sacred space, refer to Chapter Eight, but this section will give you a good starting point for understanding the process. First, think of sacred space as being like a bubble that surrounds a room. This bubble not only keeps out unwanted energy but keeps your magical power firmly in place until you're ready to direct it toward your goal.

Different magical traditions typically have different ways of creating this sphere. Most Neo-Wiccans, however, call upon the four quarters (the powers of Earth, Air, Fire, and Water) and the God and Goddess for protective assistance. To "call" a quarter simply means to invite that spiritual energy to join and help you.

The calling of the quarters usually starts in the east where the Sun rises. There are reasons you might not wish to begin there (discussed in Chapter Eight), but right now we'll go with the standard operating procedure. As you invoke each quarter, you move to that part of the room. In your mind's eye, you might visualize each point connected by a bright, white light of energy. This reinforces the effect.

Here is a sample invocation:

[Standing in or near the East and lighting a yellow or white candle.] Welcome Powers of the East and Air, the winds of change, the hope of a new day. Come join me in this sacred space to guide and protect my magic.

[Standing in or near the South and lighting a red or orange candle.] Welcome Powers of the South and Fire, the light of truth, the spark of spiritual energy. Come join me in this sacred space to guide and protect my magic.

[Standing in or near the West and lighting a blue or green candle.] Welcome Powers of the West and Water, the waves of understanding and health. Come join me in this sacred space to guide and protect my magic.

[Standing in or near the North and lighting a brown or dark green candle.] Welcome Powers of the North and Earth, the soil of growth and good foundations. Come join me in this sacred space to guide and protect my magic.

[Standing in the center, possibly at the altar, and lighting a white candle.] Welcome Spirit, that which binds the quarters together. Come join me in this sacred space to bless, guide, and protect my magic.

Now you're ready to work. Bear in mind this step isn't a requirement. It's just helpful. Sacred space increases the overall positive energy around you, which your Book of Shadows absorbs. This sphere also places a spiritual shield between you and outside influences that could detract or distract from what you're trying to accomplish. In other words, it's a great help, but not always necessary if you don't have the time or the right circumstances available.

When?

I've always been of the opinion that nearly any time is the right time for magic. Nonetheless, your schedule probably gets pretty busy between school, home, extracurriculars, chores, and friends. That means you'll want to set aside some time specifically for working on your Book of Shadows and studying your Craft—I suggest minimally once a week, but you'll have to gauge this according to your own pace. Just know that magic isn't a shake-and-bake proposition. It requires time and patience. The more attention you give to the task, the better your results!

Besides setting aside some time regularly, you can consider choosing this time frame so that it's astrologically beneficial. Our ancestors felt that timing was an important part of nearly every process. They used the Moon phases, the positions of the Sun, and the placement of the stars and planets to influence and support whatever process they were doing. While this seems like an odd idea at first, consider what happens to people every time there's a full moon or when Mercury goes retrograde. In the first case, emotions tend to run high and people are more prone to moments of lunacy (named directly for the moon's influence). In the second case, it seems like every form of communication goes awry (Mercury rules over communication). So, if Mercury is retrograde, I don't suggest working on your Book of Shadows or engaging in that conversation about magic with your folks!

When it comes to looking to the ancient astrologers for a little assistance, here are some examples of information on utilizing specific phases of the Moon, Moon signs, and the characteristics of weekdays to empower your efforts:

- **A waxing to full moon:** This time stresses personal and spiritual growth (also the increase of any specific type of positive energy). The only time you might want to consider using the waning to dark moon for your Book of Shadows is when you're writing up banishings or turnings.
- **Moon in Cancer:** The Cancer Moon supports creativity and awareness.
- **Moon in Libra:** This Moon helps keep your Book of Shadows balanced so that it reflects both your spiritual life and mundane reality.
- **Moon in Capricorn:** This is the best time to work on very personal issues, as a Moon in Capricorn stresses self-truth.
- **Moon in Sagittarius:** This is an excellent sign for working on goals. If you feel like you've been dragging your feet, now's a great time to pull out your Book.
- **Wednesday:** Pull out your Book today if you're doing something really creative (like making paper).

- **Thursday:** If you find you've had trouble getting your words down on paper and having them make sense, Thursday's energy stresses order and understanding.
- **Sunday:** This is a good day to review what you've completed so that you have time to internalize it all. There's a lot of information that you'll be putting into your Book, but if it never makes it into your heart and spirit, the time is pretty much wasted!

Now, please don't get too hung up on this. Since magic works outside of time and space, the whole timing issue is highly symbolic. When a spell says, "the best time to cast this is 2 a.m.," my response is to say, "It's 2 a.m. somewhere in the world right now!" So, think of astrological timing as an "add-on" option for those occasions when you want extra supportive energy.

Personal Preparation

I should mention at this point that the location in which you work isn't half so important as your attitude when you're working. You should wait to put together your Book of Shadows until you're well rested, in a good mood, and feel really jazzed about getting started. That upbeat energy carries over into your work, and you need not stop there. I usually wash my hands before I start working to get rid of any unwanted energies that accumulate from objects or people I've recently touched (not to mention just normal stress). I want my personal Book of Shadows to vibrate with a unique spiritual fingerprint, not a whole bunch of static, and this strategy works well for me. Give it a try!

Next, consider reserving a special outfit to wear only for spiritual purposes. No, it doesn't have to be a robe.

To be honest, my favorite choice of magical attire is a sarong. I have several, in various colors and patterns. Before a spell or ritual, I choose one that matches the goal of my magic. So, don't worry about getting a whole new wardrobe here, just find something special that somehow puts you in the right frame of mind—something that feels, well, witchy!

As you change from your everyday clothing, realize that you're switching roles. This is the point at which you become your own Priest or Priestess and put on the cloak of magic (with the new clothing). Don't let the title of Priest or Priestess put you off. It has been said that we are not humans looking for a spiritual experience, but we are spiritual beings looking for a human experience. That means you already utilize the inner Priest or Priestess each time you make an ethical choice. The only difference is that this time you purposefully move into becoming that spiritually oriented person. You are reclaiming your power!

This is a good moment to pause briefly. Allow the worries from your day to fade away. Focus your mind and heart on this moment and be wholly in it. Take several deep, calming breaths (at least three), letting the end of one breath naturally connect to the beginning of the next. Do this each time you approach working on your Book, so it becomes a familiar mini-ritual that automatically turns your mind toward magic.

If this particular approach doesn't make sense to you, try to find some type of pattern to follow that does. Why? Because humans are ritualistic. We look for comfort and familiarity in a routine, including spiritual ones. In this case, the pattern you're making creates a channel of intention through which your magical energy then flows more smoothly and successfully.

Modes and Mediums

Okay, your space is ready, and you are ready. Now we can get down to some serious work! Before we launch into all the modes and mediums, ask yourself if you have a lot of time to make something elaborate and if you have the talent to bring handcrafts into your project. I happen to be artistically challenged, so I often buy pre-made parts for my Book (like handmade paper) and add them to the whole. If you're like me and require simplicity, I advocate for three-ring binders, a bound blank book with an attractive cover, or even a digital notebook on your computer or tablet as a good place to keep things. Those who have more artistic tendencies can consider decoupage covers, hand-painted pages, making their own paper, and using calligraphy.

By the way, if you can't do the fancy stuff, don't stress about it. Part of living the magical life is learning to accept and accentuate our talents and working toward lessening our limitations. Even the simplest medium can be made very special just by adding a little creativity. Let's take the three-ring binder as an example. With this, you can:

- Photocopy images and glue them to the cover or various parts of the Book. And while you're at it, blend your glue with some herbal oils or powdered blends that match your goals.
- Type up pages using pretty fonts and photos from the internet.
- Cut out appropriate images from old magazines and use them for a collage or to highlight different sections of the Book.
- Use elementally colored dividers inside (yellow for Air, blue for Water, green for Earth, red for Fire).

See, the base medium for your Book of Shadows need not be elaborate to be meaningful, and that's what really counts. I do, however, recommend finding ways to make as much of your Book as possible by yourself. While it's nice to have beautiful things made for us, your Book of Shadows should bear your energy signature from beginning to end. Think of this signature as a sort of astral lock. As you work on any special project and really focus on it, you're putting your energy into it. At the end of this process, you want the Book to be wholly yours—a complete reflection of your individuality and spiritual pursuits. Anyone else touching or tinkering with it will feel something like a little spark, saying, "hey, don't touch!" Why? Simply because their spiritual signature is different from yours—in other words, the Book will not "like" it when someone else handles it.

If you're looking for ways to individualize your Book of Shadows, here are some fun ideas:

Think Ink!

Thanks to crafts and other specialty stores, you can get a wide variety of colored inks to use in writing up your Book's entries. Make sure to code these colors so that they match the section of the book on which you're working. For example, if you have some pages dedicated to school spells, you might want to use some bright yellow ink to emphasize the conscious mind (since this is a little hard on the eyes, using a highlighter over another color ink might be a better idea).

You can also learn to make your own invisible ink for those parts of your book that are for your eyes only. Vinegar, onion juice, and lemon juice all dry invisibly. You can apply them using a fine paintbrush. When you want to see what's on that page just put it in front of a light or heat source (like a candle) and it appears!

For those of you adept at calligraphy, add some essential oils to your ink to personalize it. Again, choose those aromatics according to the theme of the section you're preparing. Returning to the example of school, use rosemary to improve your memory!

Pagan Paper

Speaking of ink, how about some personalized paper for your Book? Anyone can learn how to make homemade paper, but it's rather messy (and you may want to ask for parental permission first). To begin, you'll need to save up fliers, junk mail, envelopes, and other unwanted pieces of paper until you have a bundle equal in size to two full newspapers. You'll also need a food processor or blender, two tablespoons of white school glue, two and a half cups of water, several pairs of old knee-highs or pantyhose, several coat hangers, and a clothing iron. Optional ingredients for your paper include vegetable or food coloring, aromatic oils, glitter, feathers, confetti, scraps of thread and lace, tiny bits of ribbon, and powdered herbs and flowers.

Shape the coat hangers into 8 x 11-inch frames (or whatever will fit the size book you wish to create). Stretch the hose over this frame. This is what you will use to create each page. (It's a good idea to make several to save time. Otherwise, you can make only one sheet per session.)

After you've made your frames, take a third of the cut-up scrap paper and put it in the blender or food processor with the water on a high setting. Slowly add the rest of the water and paper until it's completely mixed (about five minutes). This is the point at which you can add any of the specialty ingredients I mentioned; it's better still if the ingredients are theme-oriented, like rose oil and pink food coloring for a page of love spells. Fold these into the paper mixture by hand (I like using a wooden spoon that I keep set aside just for this function). Think of it like a wand with extra attitude! And don't forget—stir clockwise when you're generating positive or growth-oriented energies and counterclockwise for banishing or diminishing energy.

Next, fill a sink with four inches of water. Put your frames in the bottom of the sink. If you want to have faintly tinted paper or gentle aromatics, add them to the water too. Pour your paper into the sink and mix it with the glue (again, use your wooden spoon for this). When it gets really thick, turn to hand-kneading it like you would bread.

Now, reach down and grasp the frame, bringing it slowly to the surface through the water (make sure it gets an even covering of paper). Set each frame aside to dry. I like using a cooling rack for this, set in a sunny window or other dry, warm location. Underneath it, I put paper towels that collect drippings and keep cleanup easier. By the way, if you run out of frames and have leftovers, freeze them in Ziploc-style bags. You can reuse this for your next batch.

Each frame has to dry completely. At this point, the paper peels away easily (keep the frames for making more sheets in the future). Put the completed sheet on an ironing board with a cloth underneath it and iron each on the high setting. This removes the last bits of water from the paper and also provides you with a flatter writing surface. Leave these flattened papers in the open air for two days before using them.

Important: You're not done yet. It's time to clean up the mess! Carefully take your remnants outside (maybe pour them into an old grocery bag) and put them in the garbage. Do not put them in the toilet or flush them down the sink as they will clog pipes.

Alternative: If your family nixes the idea of homemade paper, just buy some pleasing stationery at a store. Take a cloth that's been dabbed with a personally meaningful aromatic oil and put it in a box with the paper you've bought. Within a few weeks, the paper will absorb the aroma. From here, write up your pages and decorate them, finally protecting them with a sheet protector, lamination, or fixative art spray. Again, however, please be considerate when you're working on crafts. Put down protective paper so that countertops, rugs, and tablecloths don't get damaged.

Flower Power

I keep a lot of pressed flowers and herbs in my Book of Shadows partly in order to have ready-made spell components when I need them. I place the flower or herb in the section where its energies will do the most good. For example, in the section on "sleep," I keep a sprig of dill, historically used to encourage sleep. (In the original Norse, *dilla* means "to lull.")

If you'd like to press your own flowers and herbs, begin by picking them when they're dry (not covered in dew or rain). Gently clean off any dirt (a toothbrush or small paintbrush works well). Place the flowers or leaves on several layers of paper towels on a flat surface, taking care that they do not touch. Put more paper towels on top (or perhaps grocery bags). Now you can make another layer. When you've got an inch of paper towels and plant matter piled up, put several heavy books or a large piece of wood on the top of the pile. Leave this for six to eight weeks before you check to see if the plants are "done." If they peel off easily and feel totally dry—they're ready to go into your Book of Shadows.

Amuletic Aromatics

Speaking of flowers, what about adding aromas to your Book? Aromatherapy is very much in style right now, so you can find various essential oils in a lot of places (I've even seen them at the supermarket). Mind you, what we now call aromatherapy is really thousands of years old, and it certainly has strong ties to magic. Since around 1500 BCE, people have been using a wide variety of incense and oils as a way of improving spells or rituals and even for pleasing the Divine. Please be aware that essential oils are the pure oils of the plant and are extremely concentrated. A little goes a long way, and they should never be applied directly to the skin without diluting them in water or a safer carrier oil (like olive or coconut oil). Just be aware that most carrier oils have a shelf life of about a year, so don't go overboard!

When you'd like to add some symbolic aromas to your Book's pages, here are some ideas to get you started. I've limited this list to some of the herbs or additives you might find in your pantry so that, if need be, you can make your own infused oil. Remember, though, that if a scent means something different to you than what I've provided here, go with that meaning.

Aromatic Correspondences

- **Basil:** love, transition (especially during endings), purification, courage
- **Bay Leaves:** prophesy, spiritual awareness, physical strength and adeptness, love and romance, protection, initiation
- **Chamomile:** harmony, recuperation, peace, rest
- **Cinnamon:** protection, money, luck, warming things up
- **Dill:** good fortune, hospitality, magical studies (focusing on), restfulness
- **Ginger:** protection, healing, giving works a bit of a kick
- **Lemon:** refreshing energy, purification, and cleansing
- **Mint:** prosperity, happiness, celebration, communication, success
- **Rosemary:** memory, healing, hex-breaking, fidelity, loyalty
- **Sage:** psychic awareness, turning negativity, wisdom, self-management
- **Vanilla:** love (including self-love)

Making your own herbal-infused oils isn't too difficult, and as you work on them you can pour your intentions into the blend. Just warm some good quality carrier oil (olive oil is the easiest to find) in a pan on low heat and steep about one tablespoonful of herbs to one cup of oil. Don't boil this. Let it sit like tea. Add more if the results aren't as strong as you'd like, straining with a cheese cloth or fine sieve after every steeping. If you have a tea ball to put your herbs into, it makes it much easier and yields a very clear aromatic oil.

Store the finished oil in a dark bottle with a good lid (like those for cough syrup—cleaned out with very hot water first). Keep this in a dark, cool area and it will usually last six months to a year. If the oil gets cloudy, discard it. That means the oil's gone bad, which also destroys any magical energy you put into it originally.

The finished oils aren't only useful for dabbing on your Book. You can also use them to anoint your pulse points (so you carry that energy in your aura all day), rub them into the frame of your bed (to surround yourself with energy), or even polish various magical tools with them! Just remember to label each bottle with what it contains, any special timing you used to create it, and any special symbolism the oil has for you so you don't mix them up later.

The Graphics Genius

I can't draw to save my life. I'm pretty good, however, at finding pictures in magazines, greeting cards, postcards, and online that seem to fit nicely with the topics in my Book of Shadows. You can too! The more visual cues you give yourself, and the more those images reflect the goals of the magic on that page, the better your results become. For example, if you enjoy gardening and include a section on magical gardening methods in your Book you could support that energy by adding the image of a lush, blossoming garden to that page. This picture is not only visually appealing, but it expresses your wish or goal!

For those who like to draw or doodle, you can hand draw symbols and images in various places. Geometric shapes offer one option here because they're simple, fast, and highly symbolic. A circle, for example, represents wholeness, protection, and cycles. The square represents Earth energies (such as mundane situations or money) and the upward triangle is Fire or increasing energy. And if you're worried about using pencil, don't be. A light coat of hairspray or art fixative will keep the images from smudging or erasing easily, just make sure to let it dry fully before closing your Book.

Clever Covers

I have discovered some of the most amazing pre-made Books of Shadows both online and at local witch shops. The covers of these books leave no question as to their purpose, and they each look like an old tome that was snatched from a mage's bookshelf! Nonetheless, books like this are very expensive. So, what can you do to give your Book of Shadows a facelift without spending a fortune?

My suggestion is to cover the book in specialty paper or fabric. In either case, you can add all kinds of decorative touches to the surface using a sturdy glue. Examples include crystals, a scrying mirror (see instructions in Chapter Six for making one), and prefabricated applique (get this at most sewing shops).

Conjure up Color!

Take a moment and look at something that's the color of a clear blue sky. How does that color make you feel? Now look at something red. Do your sensations change? This is an example of how color influences our feelings, energy levels, and responses to various situations. Our witchy ancestors realized this long before modern psychologists did and ascribed specific characteristics to each color.

Here is a brief list for your reference:

- **Red:** The color of the Fire element (South of the Sacred Circle) that represents power, energy, passion, bravery, health, and stamina.
- **Orange:** A gentler form of Fire that represents the harvest, our will, awareness, and friendship.
- **Yellow (Gold):** The traditional color of the Air element (East), representing sun magic, blessings, communication, leadership, logic, and the God aspect.
- **Green:** The color of the Earth (North) that represents wellness, growth, and progress.
- **Blue:** The Water element (West) that represents peace or joy, honesty, and dream work.
- **Purple:** Represents spiritual matters, wisdom, theoretical learning, and the inner world (internalizing what you learn).
- **Black:** Represents rest, completion, closure, banishing, and the Goddess aspect.
- **White:** A lunar color symbolizing protection, purity, and the God aspect.
- **Brown:** Another earthly hue for putting down roots, foundations, and grounding energy.
- **Gray:** The color of neutrality, uncertainty, choices, and transformation. Gray stands between day and night, positive and negative energy.

If a color has a meaning different from these for you because of personal experience, always trust yourself. No one else is going to be using your personal Book of Shadows unless you share it, and even then, it's still your book. You're the one who needs to have a strong emotional and mental connection to all the decorative touches you place inside.

By the way, if you don't want to use colored ink or paper for some reason, there are other ways to use color when making your Book of Shadows. You can dress in a specific color (or colors) to literally "put on" the associated energy, put a tinted light bulb in a lamp near where you're working so it diffuses the energy, put a colored wax seal on a page (even better if the imprint on the seal has meaning), or have a snack handy that's the right color for your goal. For example, carrots are a great snack for when you want to work on the psychic section of your Book. They're not only the right color but represent the "sight" on a spiritual level. And, being a root vegetable, they also help keep you grounded while you work.

Digital Delights

My handwriting is nearly as lousy as my artwork, so typing things out and then printing and pasting them into my Book of Shadows is much easier. This also allows for some basic graphic design when selecting fonts and images that align with the information you're working on. For example, if you've created a Book that has a nice leather cover and looks a bit like it's an antique, you can pick a fancier font with some old-school illustrations to really home in on that particular vibe within your Book as well.

There are also a lot of fabulous journaling apps out there that allow you to both insert photos and handwrite sections of your book—many of which also sync with your phone! One of the benefits of this is that it becomes much easier to reference previous sections within your work without having to carry around a large, decorated tome.

I'm sure as you read this list you'll come up with even more ideas of your own. Make note of them! I have seen some of the most amazing Books of Shadows and other magical tools produced by young adults just because they're open to new ideas and really enjoy self-expression. So long as you're happy with the final look and feel of the Book, you've done a great job!

Purposeful Patterning

And what about using various patterns to convey a message? Why not? After all, the media uses symbols all the time, as do artists, to convey a certain feeling. Here's a list of shapes and their symbolic value for your consideration:

- **Almond:** spiritual energy, often that of the God/dess
- **Anchor:** firm foundations, protection, safe harbor
- **Ankh:** the Egyptian symbol of life
- **Arrow:** movement, reaching a goal, direction
- **Circle:** safety, the border between the worlds, unity, wholeness
- **Crescent:** lunar magic, protection, vitality
- **Cross (equidistant):** the four Elements in perfect balance
- **Equal sign:** balance, symmetry, justice
- **Eye:** vision, both physical and spiritual insight
- **Heart:** your emotional nature
- **Key:** openings and opportunities
- **Knot:** holding specific energy in place
- **Stairs:** movement (often upward)
- **Line:** self-awareness, self-actualization
- **Peace sign:** end to hostility
- **Spiral:** energy in motion (inward for the self, outward for manifestation)
- **Square:** Earth magic, mundane issues (money, daily reality)
- **Square and Circle Superimposed:** opposites (the meeting of the dimensions and worlds—mundane and

magical, temporal and eternal)
- **Star:** wishes
- **Triangle (point up):** fire magic, the conscious mind, and the God aspect
- **Triangle (point down):** decreasing energies, banishing, the subconscious

You can utilize these as doodles on specific pages of your Book of Shadows, as part of the cover, or even in charms and ritual work! For example, you might create your personal sacred space in an oval shape (you can still have the four quarters of an oval) to honor the Goddess if you want to work with that feminine energy. Or, when you need a more rational way of seeing a situation, carry a triangular piece of fluorite as a charm to connect you with the God and logical energies.

What to Put in Your Book of Shadows

Okay, you now know how to put together your Book so that it's meaningful and filled with personal energy. The next question becomes, what exactly goes in a Book of Shadows in the way of materials? I mean, this is basically like a Bible for witches, so the contents are pretty important.

The first question to ask yourself is, what type of magical processes and components do you think you'll use most often? Those are among the first things you'll want to add to your Book, simply so you have the information handy all the time. The second question is how much space will you need for each section of your Book. This is especially important to people who are using a pre-bound diary. It really sucks when you have this beautifully decorated, well-thought-out section only to discover you didn't leave enough space for everything and have to skip ahead and put the rest elsewhere. Sometimes I think it's better to have several bound Books—one for each subject—so this doesn't happen. The third important question is, how many topics do you want in your Book? To be honest, my Book of Shadows is on my computer. Here's a list of the files that I keep:

- Magical Tools
- Meditations
- Sacred Space
- Portable Magic
- Prayers
- Visualizations
- Spellcraft
- Annual Celebrations
- Elemental Magic
- Color Correspondence
- Aromatics
- Crystals, Metals, and Minerals
- God and Goddesses
- Favorite Books (with notes)
- Rituals
- Networking Notes
- Children's Activities
- Notable People in Magic
- Techno Magic
- Divination Methods
- Ghosts and Hauntings
- Candle Magic
- Holistic Health
- Fire Circles
- Labyrinths and Mandalas
- Herbal Recipes
- Mythical Creatures

- Magical Paths (described)
- Altar Ideas (by theme/season)
- Moon Magic
- Witchy History and Mythology
- Gardening
- Animal Magic
- Favorite Quotes
- Dream Work
- Kitchen Magic
- Numerology
- Potions
- Spiritual Diary
- Festivals and Gatherings
- Glossary of Terms
- Online Resources
- Music and Artists
- Psychic Exercises
- Sacred Sites
- Drumming and Dancing
- Plant Correspondences
- Folklore and Superstition
- Global Celebrations
- Magical Self-Defense
- Planetary Magic
- Symbolism (pictorial)
- Handcrafts

From this list, you can see why I keep it on my computer! I like things separated so I can find what I want, when I want it. For people using a three-ring binder or diary-style Book, I recommend having a table of contents or colored tabs to keep things separated and user-friendly. In any case, you'll have to decide the best way to organize things for yourself and what to include. Once you take that step, you can then start the process of gathering information (no small task either!).

Exactly where you find your information is up to you. Begin with your favorite books, a spiritual teacher, or perhaps watch a documentary (which often has great information on magic, witches, and New Age ideologies). Find information online or take notes when you go to a gathering or take a class. Wherever you find good material, however, make sure you note the source. You may want to return to it again for more information or recommend it to a friend interested in the Craft.

By the way, don't write your notes immediately in your Book. Instead, I recommend typing or writing them on notebook paper and then taking your time to transfer them over later. This accomplishes two things. First, you get rid of the dross—stuff you already have accumulated or don't need. Second, it allows you to read over all the material and look for the best of it. You don't want to keep anything in here that gets outdated quickly, and you also want to put the transferred information into the section where it makes sense. For example, if you find a great recipe for an herbal potion, it could go under "Herbs" or "Potions" or both. Decide where you'll find it the most easily.

Finally, I should mention that your Book of Shadows is like a magical map of sorts. It's going to continue to expand outward as your understanding of the magical world expands. That's really the fun part about this. You can go back to your very first book in a few years and enjoy everything there, but also appreciate how much you've changed.

Storing Your Book and Tools

A lot of witches like to have a special place in which to keep their Book of Shadows or magical tools, and some also like to have special coverings for them as well. When anyone other than you handles these items (even your pets), the energy imprint in them is changed, and not always for the better. By keeping your Book and tools in a safe place, you protect them from curious hands and paws, not to mention any damage that could be done by either.

Where might you want to store such items? For a while, I used my cedar hope chest. It was perfect, with lots of room to spare. Another option (and far less costly) is a large plastic tub (with a well-fitting lid). This slides neatly into closets or under your bed when you're not using it. Note: this shouldn't be used to hide anything from your family but rather to protect the tools of your Craft (see Chapter One).

As far as coverings go, stick with natural fabrics. Cotton, wool, and linen are three good choices. Many witches like using white cloth since that's the color of pure intention and protection, but that's purely a personal decision (I prefer purple, personally). For storing small items like a tarot deck, you might want to consider a wooden box or pouch instead of a loose cloth that can easily slide off. I like wooden boxes because they're more waterproof (and tarot decks aren't very forgiving of spilled soda).

Basically, you just want to treat your Book of Shadows and your magical tools with the respect they're due. Proper care and keeping are part of that treatment that also neatly keeps your treasured items away from dust, dirt, and other possible damaging agents.

Book Blessing

I said earlier that your Book of Shadows is really never done because humans never stop growing and changing until we leave our bodies. Even so, there are moments that we reach in the process of creating our Book of Shadows where the work seems as complete as it can be. This is an excellent time to consider blessing your book.

Before you get nervous about this idea, know that blessing is simply a way of setting apart your Book for its purpose. A blessing, in whatever form you choose, protects the material within and removes any random chaotic energy that might have been absorbed throughout the creation process. When you bless your Book, it simply makes it a little more harmonious and complete.

In nearly every world faith, blessing includes some type of hand motion. In Neo-Paganism, people most often turn their hands palm-downward above (or on) the Book. The palm of the hand is a place through which universal energy can flow easily. It helps to visualize a sparkling white light that pours down like the Sun from above, into your head, and down through your arm. This imagery may make you feel a little tingly or warm—if so, you're doing it right!

At this point, you can call on your vision of a God or Goddess to empower the work of your hands. Or you might call on the Guardians of the Earth to come together and fill its pages with their special form of magic. Here's one example of a blessing to try:

I stand in the circle. In a time-not-time. In a place-not-place. And seek blessings.
From the Power of the Air—I ask that the words in this book communicate the truths I discover

> *with clarity and that they never become stale and lifeless.*
>
> *From the Power of Fire—I seek a passion to learn my art and the inner light with which to read all that's placed herein with an open mind.*
>
> *From the Power of Water—I ask for intuitiveness to fill each dot and point so that magic flows from these pages into my spirit.*
>
> *From the Power of Earth—I seek strong foundations in which my Craft will take root and grow.*
>
> *By my will, with Divine blessing! As it has been said, So let it be!*

Feel free to change these words in any way that makes you comfortable or, better yet, make up your own blessing! You might as well get used to taking the steering wheel back in your spiritual car from the beginning of this book because I'll continue to challenge you to do so. I'm only the driving instructor, after all!

Chapter III

Getting Started

Spiritual practices are called "practices" for a reason. Like so many other areas of life (even if it sounds cliché), practice really does make perfect. You're not going to become an adept witch overnight, nor by reading any one book. It takes a little time to get to know your tools and methods. And, if you want your magic to work consistently, you have to invest a little effort and learn good techniques.

To get you off on the right foot, this chapter explores the customary tools of witchcraft. It also supplies simple activities to help hone your willpower and focus, two things on which your Craft relies heavily. Please be patient with yourself as you try these. Progress can sometimes be slow. Other times, it may seem like nothing is happening because the real transformation isn't external, it's inside you. Remember that you're effectively "exercising" your spirit in a way that it's unaccustomed to. Just like a muscle you haven't used before, you'll find your magical power grows in direct relation to how frequently it gets a good workout. So, let's hit the metaphysical gym!

The Witch Within

Witchcraft isn't an elite club or social group. It's open to everyone who finds that the methods and ideals help them be the best person they can be. Even so, people often ask me if they can become a witch without having anyone in their family who was one, or without any special gifts. The answer is yes, absolutely!

For one thing, every person has gifts. They need not be flashy to be useful and very important spiritually. Things like kindness, thoughtfulness, and helpfulness—these are all gifts that also have real-life applications and manifestations! So, you need not be psychic or have a family tradition of witchery to become a witch. I certainly didn't, nor did many of our community's current leaders. Instead, they simply discovered the witch within and then began nurturing that magical being. You can too.

So, if you've decided you'd like to walk down this path a little way and see what's waiting, what's the next step? Well, besides having two willing hands and a heart full of love, magic requires a substantial amount of willpower and focus. These two things are tied together, but I'd like to examine them separately with you for a moment.

The dictionary defines the human will as the mind taking control over its own operations. Here, your thoughts determine, resolve, decree, or command a specific outcome. In terms of your magic, will is the driving force for manifestation, so what happens in your mind during a magical process is very important (that's where focus ties in). The power to make and change reality truly begins with but a thought.

Now, I don't know about you, but my willpower isn't always as strong or sure as I might like. That lack, unfortunately, hinders the flow of magic. So, exactly what type of willpower does magic require? The best way to describe effective willpower for any metaphysical process is to think of a stubborn five-year-old holding tightly to a wish. The child doesn't know that the wish might be impossible, and he or she wouldn't care if someone said otherwise!

Instead, the child willfully demands that this wish get attention. Now, while magic is a lot more mature and respectful than the five-year-old child's demeanor, the example is still useful. You need to have that kind of resolve about what you want to accomplish. Believe it can happen, trust in it. In your mind's eye, see it as already fulfilled!

Will-Building Process

Determine your goal in detail (don't overlook small points, they're important).

Know why you want this goal to manifest, how you'd like it to manifest, when everything needs to happen, and other important details.

Take a moment to meditate about your goal. Turn it over in your mind and examine it from all angles, including how it may affect others. Remember, what we think we want and need isn't always what we really want and need.

When you're certain you have the goal fleshed out, add some affirmations to the process. An affirmation is simply a positive sentence that states the goal as realized. For example, if you want success, start saying out loud, "I am successful." This accomplishes two things. First, your words vibrate throughout your energetic body, changing the patterns there to attract and welcome success. Second, your mind is focusing (yep, there's that word again) on the goal as you speak about it.

Put the affirmation into motion. I often find that dancing or power walking while I speak affirmations increases my determination. Movement generates power that you can channel into your will. When you hear your own words and know that they're true and valid, your will is ready for magic.

Okay, so you're all pumped up and feeling very assured. Now what? The next thing you'll need (other than any tools and components for the process) is focus. From beginning to end, you need to keep your mind centered on that one goal. Concentrate on it, and don't shift your awareness. That's why I often recommend turning off your phone and finding a quiet, private place to work. Distractions often derail your focus (even experienced witches find that's true). If you live in a noisy neighborhood or home, earplugs work wonders when you can't get alone time.

There are a variety of ways to teach yourself how to focus effectively. One is to take an object like a crystal and set it down on a plain surface (a black cloth works very well). Put one facet of the crystal so it faces you. Now look at it. Note every detail you can from this angle. Don't let your eyes stray to other things in the room. Center your attention wholly on that one object, then turn the crystal slightly. Do you notice differences in the angles, the colors, the shapes, and the overall feeling of the crystal? If you do, you've got a good grasp of focus. Practice this exercise for five minutes at first, then slowly increase the amount of time you spend focusing so that, eventually, you can maintain your concentration through an entire ritual. How long is that? I recommend about sixty to ninety minutes. Most rituals don't go much longer than that.

Another good way to improve your focus is by meditating. To meditate means to reflect on (or review) something in your mind, much as you might ponder a difficult question on an exam. Thinking deeply and clearly about any particular topic (including a goal) helps bring your ideas and beliefs onto the same stage. More importantly, it's a stage on which your mind and spirit are far less busy—the goal being to teach yourself to think about one thing at a time and grasp that one item fully, rather than the hundreds of functions your brain does simultaneously (talk about multitasking!). Meditation also has a great side effect: It benefits your willpower. Thoughts have very viable energy, and when we understand something fully, we can put a lot more positive magic into it!

Every day, you're surrounded by thousands of sights, sounds, and other sensory input. This keeps your thoughts pretty occupied—often too occupied to really focus or build will. In fact, some days probably feel like a whirlwind. Meditation takes all that activity, calms it down, and, in turn, provides a stress-free atmosphere where you can really look at things differently, like a movie in your mind. From this perspective, you can see the bigger picture with greater detachment.

But a lot of people that I meet have trouble with meditation. It takes time for your mind to learn how to turn away all those other random thoughts that it's used to handling. It also takes practice to get used to sitting still for more than a few minutes at a time! So, if you're feeling frustrated by meditation, you need to be patient with yourself here. Try this ten-step process and see if it helps. If it does, put it into your Book of Shadows to use again!

Ten-Step Meditation Process

Start out slowly. Try meditating for only a couple minutes at first (say five). Each day, increase that time a little bit. This allows you to get used to extended periods of purposeful focusing at a pace that's reasonable.

Get up a little early each day. Experts tell us that the first thing in the morning is the best time to get good results from your meditation efforts. The next best alternative time is right before dinner.

Sit in a comfortable position. Nope—no need to look like a pretzel. In fact, people often walk, dance, or exercise while meditating!

Stretch out a bit so that nothing feels uncomfortable. Your body is among the most difficult obstacles to overcome in meditation as sitting still isn't something most people do well.

Close your eyes and take a nice, deep breath. Let go of any tension or worries. Try to just be in this moment.

Now, slow your breathing down a bit. Keep the pace slow and even so that one breath naturally leads to the next without any interruptions. It sometimes helps to imagine your breath filled with white light. In your mind's eye, you can see each breath making a circle in through your nose, and out through your mouth.

When you feel calm and centered, direct your mind to the meditation's goal (or an issue/situation about which you want to see more clearly).

Direct your attention wholly to that item. Let it play out in your mind completely. Continue until you feel like you know it inside out and backwards, until you feel like it's part of you. Note that your first few times trying meditation, you may not get this far. That's fine. Just bear in mind that until you reach this point, you won't be able to really utilize meditation for anything other than improving your ability to focus for longer periods.

Once you feel as if you've accomplished all you can, start returning your breathing pace to normal and slowly open your eyes. I don't recommend standing up or moving quickly as that often results in a headache or feelings of dizziness. Just sit still for a few minutes and let yourself return to center.

While you're grounding, write down any important insights gained from the meditative time in your Book of Shadows or a magical diary. These may prove very helpful to you later when creating a spell or ritual for that subject, or when dealing with that situation.

Most people find that the first time they meditate, even a few minutes can seem to take forever. The better you become at meditation, the faster the time seems to go by. I also recommend setting a quiet alarm on your phone as a gentle reminder to finish so you're not late for school or other tasks and appointments!

Until you have a little more experience with meditating regularly, you may find that you get uncomfortable quickly, notice every last itch or tickle, or get distracted by even the tiniest noises. That's perfectly normal, as it's your mind's way of struggling with the exercise you're giving it. To offset that difficulty, try burning incense, playing some soft music, or chanting. These provide some external sensual stimuli that occupy part of your mind so that the majority of it can be directed to the task at hand. In time, you won't need those external supports, but you may want to use them anyway if they improve your results.

Tools of the Trade

Willpower and vision create the inner foundations for all your external magical workings. Once you begin getting a handle on those two things, the next step in witchcraft is getting to know what tools witches typically use, why we use them, and which ones work best for you. There are a wide variety of items in the traditional witch's kit, not to mention a bunch of personal, creative ones! We'll review them here in alphabetical order so you can find information quickly when you need it.

Before I do, however, I'd like to take a moment to stress that tools aren't necessary to your art. They're only an external symbol of something that's happening internally in your mind and spirit. Ultimately, if all you have is a keen mind and two good hands, you've really got everything you need. Tools just make the job a little easier because they act as a conduit for our intention and energy. Confidence doesn't develop overnight. It takes time and practice until the tool becomes simply an extension of the self—one that makes your job a little easier.

Here's a list of common tools, their symbolic value, and uses in magic. You may want to preface various parts of your Book of Shadows with some of this information so it's handy when you need it.

Animal Symbols

Our forebears felt that every animal had specific powers and that by using or wearing animal parts one could capture those powers. For example, a lion represents strength and vocal power. So, carrying a lion's tooth or claw would grant the bearer those same abilities.

While our ancestors often used actual animal parts in their magic, modern witches recognize the need to act in partnership with nature and protect it. Therefore, most stick to using animal symbols, which I'm sure your parents will appreciate! Things like small figurines and pictures from magazines come immediately to mind as perfect substitutes for actual parts.

So, how might you utilize these symbolic items? In spellcraft, carrying an energized image acts like a charm or amulet that continually releases the energies desired into and around your space. For example, when you're dealing with a hectic schedule, a bee image that's been charged and blessed might be ideal. Other potential applications include:

- Setting images of various animals around the sacred space so that their spiritual energy guards and protects.
- Directing energy toward the image of an animal you know is endangered or ill.
- Visualizing a specific animal in your meditations to encourage that energy in your life.
- Placing the image of an animal on your altar to honor a deity. Many gods and goddesses had sacred animals, like the Egyptian goddess Bast, whose animal was the cat.
- Observing animals for omens and signs of things to come. The ancients took particular note of any unusual animal meeting or movement and pondered its potential meaning according to the creature's symbolic value. For example, a random sighting of a mole in an area where they don't usually go might portend the need to dig down and make yourself less visible or get to the "roots" of a situation.

I should also mention that many witches have a live animal companion that they consider to be a magical partner and helpmate. Mine's a cat named Butler. Most often these animals find you, and you'll recognize them by their ongoing interest in your magic. Should such a creature bless your life, be thankful and treat the animal with great love and respect. This is not merely a "pet" —it is a spiritual partner.

Just For Fun: Animal Holidays and Festivals

For those of you wondering what global festivals and holidays integrate animals, there are hundreds. You can look to these dates for enacting spells or rituals when you want to connect with a specific type of animal energy or honor a guide that's come into your life. Returning to the previous example of a bee—if this is your spirit helper, you might do something special to commemorate that connection during late August (the freeing of the insects festival—Japan).

- **Bat Flight Breakfast** *(Second Thursday in August, Carlsbad Caverns, New Mexico, US)*: An event created to observe bat movements and educate people on their habitat and characteristics.
- **Be Kind to Animals Week** *(First week in May, US)*: A full week dedicated to helping animals and humane societies.
- **Carabao Festival** *(Third week in May, Philippines)*: A lively festival to honor St. Isidro Labrador, the patron of Filipino farmers. All beasts of burden are decorated and blessed by a parish priest.
- **Excited Insects Day** *(March 5, China)*: Today is when insects and other natural beings are honored, along

with the earth's fertility. Typically, farmers sow rice and wheat today, while others lay flowers on the graves of ancestors, welcoming spring and the insects and other animals who come out from hibernation.

- **Festival of the Cow** *(January 25, San Pablo de los Montes)*: A Christianized pagan festival that was intended to inspire providence, prosperity, and blessings.
- **Freeing the Insects** *(Late August-early September, Japan)*: During this time of year, various insects kept as pets during the year are freed in parks and shrines for good luck.
- **Groundhog Day** *(February 2, US)*: This is the day on which a groundhog is said to predict the weather.
- **Kartika Purnima** *(Full moon in either October or November; India)*: Hindu celebration of the day when God incarnated in fish form. Bathing in the river Ganges or other holy water is traditional on this day.
- **Kattestoet** *(Second Sunday in May, Belgium)*: This special festival for cats features people dressed in feline costumes and street parades displaying figurines such as Bast.
- **Keretkun Festival** *(Late autumn, Siberia)*: This festival honors the sea animals on which northern people depend for many mundane things. During the celebration, symbolic representations of the animals killed during hunting season are returned to the waters to replenish nature's storehouse and thus ensure plentiful future seasons.
- **Mid-Autumn Festival** *(On or near September 15, China)*: The story goes that the Chinese, when looking to the dark side of the Moon, saw a rabbit that knew the secrets of immortality. This festival commemorates that rabbit's birthday, and pet rabbits are often sold in the streets to ensure the buyer's longevity.

- **Nativity of the Virgin** *(September 8, Germany):* Traditionally people bring their horses to St. Margen today to be blessed by a priest.
- **Pooram** *(April–May, India):* This Hindu celebration honoring Shiva includes the displaying of temple elephants ridden by the Brahmans in ornamental regalia.
- **St. Francis of Assisi Day** *(October 3–4, Europe):* This Saint was considered a guardian of all animals. Typically, people have their pets blessed on this day.
- **Songkran** *(April 12–14, Thailand):* A celebration featuring water blessings, during which captive birds and fish are freed to encourage happiness and good health. Note that a similar festival, called Thingyan, is held in Burma in mid-April.
- **Tihar** *(October–November, Nepal):* Each day of this festival honors different animals, beginning with crows, cows, then dogs (who are friends in the afterlife), oxen, and bullocks. Participants in this festival are insured luck and the blessings of Lakshmi.
- **Ute Bear Dance** *(Memorial Day weekend, Colorado, US):* This festival of the Ute people honors the bear's reawakening after hibernation. The dancers gain power from the Bear spirit at this event, for health in particular.

Tools of the Trade

Animal symbols are tools. Here are the other tools you'll want to know about, along with some general tips and instructions.

Asperger

This is just a fancy word for anything that you use to sprinkle water around sacred space to get rid of unwanted energies. I've used feathers, leaves, brooms, and bundles of flowers for this purpose. If you wish, you can add a few drops of aromatic oil to the water for more symbolic value. For example, if your spell or ritual is focused on helping you with schoolwork, add a few drops of rosemary (to improve memory and support the conscious mind).

Athame

Okay, this one won't likely become part of your parents' Yule list. An athame is a sacred dagger that witches use ceremonially. The traditional blade of an athame has two edges, one of which represents the good our magic can do, and one the harm it can do. This is a very powerful representation, and one that gives us a good reason to stop and think about our motives before releasing any magical energy.

Alternatively, or simultaneously, the athame can represent the God aspect. Just as the cauldron and cup represent the feminine powers of the universe, the dagger, sword, and wand of the witch give equal time to the masculine powers. In a world where gender tends to be overly stressed, I think this balance is very important. We're reminded here that people are people—all have value, and all are sacred.

In spells and rituals, witches may outline the sacred circle and direct energy into that outline using the athame. You can visualize a brilliant white light shooting out from the point of the dagger so that it draws a circle of power. Another use for an athame is to point the way for magic to follow (as when you release a spell). Also, a High Priest or Priestess may use the athame to cut a way into or out of a sacred space for a member who arrives late or must leave unexpectedly.

Since many parents will be a little antsy about their child having one of these, especially a sharp one, I propose several alternatives. First would be a decorative athame made from unsharpened stone. The second would be to use your finger or even a butter knife. A third good option is a simple wooden wand (a tree twig) that you've decorated in a special manner. I like this option because it comes from nature and you can choose both the wood and the decoration according to specific magical needs and goals.

Making a Wand

If you'd like to make a wand, it's not overly difficult. Find a twig outside that's about twelve inches long, preferably one with little knotholes into which you can put crystals and shells. Soak this in warm water for several days to loosen the bark. Remove it and lay it on some newspaper. Rub the bark off using rough sandpaper. As the bark gets thinner, go to a softer grade of sandpaper so you don't gouge the wood underneath.

Once the wand is smooth, look for spots to put small stones. Glue these in using a good wood glue or epoxy. Wrap a piece of cloth around one end (the end you'll hold in your hand) and secure it by crisscrossing a ribbon from the top downward. Knot the ribbon and leave some extra at the end (You might want to hang beads or feathers from this.).

When you're done, treat the wand with lemon or orange oil to keep the wood from cracking. You should retreat it every couple of months (or any time the wood looks or feels dry).

Broom

The original brooms (or *besoms*) were made from the broom plant, a very stalky bit of greenery that yields numerous branches, ideal for bundling on the end of a stick. By the time the Romans came into power, brooms were already connected with magical arts, and they were used in various ways in numerous Pagan traditions. People jumped over a broom for luck or as part of a wedding, for example.

Since most people have a broom in the pantry, this is still a particularly accessible tool. Use it like a wand or to sweep the circle rather than using an asperger. On New Year's or your birthday, sweep out the old energies and then sweep in the new! And it is perfectly okay to use a vacuum cleaner instead. I often like to utilize this tool to gather up unwanted energy in my home. First, I'll sprinkle some rug freshener out (to lift the energy), then chant or sing while I sweep to bring joy to the room. On top of the positive magical effect, you'll be getting a chore done and making your folks very happy!

Candles

In many cultures, the light of a candle represents a person's soul, the presence of Spirit, and enlightenment. This is certainly still true in magic. Witches often place candles on their altars to honor a god or goddess, but the usefulness of this household item doesn't stop there.

Candles are one of the simplest and cheapest components of spellcraft. Pick a candle whose color represents your goal (like green for money). Carve an emblem in it (like a dollar sign) and dab it with an aromatic oil (like mint, which encourages prosperity) and you're all set to go! Ask a parent's permission before using candles and try to find self-enclosed candles for safety.

Removing Candle Wax

One of the major problems witches often have is the fact that candle drippings end up on robes, altar cloths, and sometimes rugs. If this happens, you can still redeem things. Use an ice cube to freeze off as much of the wax as possible. Next, put several layers of newspaper on top of the wax. Warm an iron to the lowest setting. Iron the paper, removing the bottom layer as it absorbs the melted wax. Continue in this manner until all the wax is out of the fabric.

In a ritual setting, candles are often set at the four quarters. Specifically, a red or orange one goes in the South for Fire, a blue or purple one in the West for Water, a green or brown one in the North for Earth, and a yellow or white one in the East for Air. These are lit during opening invocations as the witch walks the circle, welcoming those powers.

Finally, candles and wax drippings both have been used by witches for divination. I will cover this topic in more detail in Chapter Six. If your parents nix the idea of candles, you can use colored light bulbs or LED candles instead. In this case, dab just a little aromatic oil on them and turn it on to "light up" the magic!

Cauldron

You can often find me in my kitchen stirring a big old pot of soup or stew, which makes me laugh at the stereotype I've just become. Nonetheless, such pots have been central to the witch's Craft for a very long time. Within Neo-Wicca, the classic cauldron symbolizes the threefold Goddess (Maiden, Mother, and Crone) because of its three legs and the womblike shape of the bowl.

In the context of modern magic, cauldrons of all sizes find their way into sacred space. Some may hold incense, being fire-safe containers. Some may hold water, flowers, or other symbolic items that visually emphasize the theme of the magic. Others still might be the simmering point for the after-ritual meal! I personally just keep a small one on my altar and fill it with seasonal components for spells.

Costumes, Masks, and Robes

There is a good reason for the theatrical quality to most magical methods. When we watch a movie or a play, we often suspend our sense of the concrete reality around us, which in turn allows for that movie or play's reality to blossom in our imagination. Similarly, by putting on costumes, masks, and other items different from everyday wear, we begin to transport ourselves away from mundane thinking.

Let's put this idea in the context of our ancestors' times for a minute. Here, you have a tribe of people who know each other very well. At the time of a ritual, the spiritual leader may don special clothing and a mask that honored a spirit. Now, instead of this same guy you've seen every day all your life by the light of the fire, you see an impressive figure dancing and chanting. This, in turn, conveys a strong impression to the participant's mind, especially the subconscious. It is still the same for us today.

In the case of modern settings, robes and special jewelry are probably the most popular accoutrements. These might be chosen to represent the season by their colors or patterns or perhaps the theme of the gathering. But really, unless you belong to a group that asks for special clothing, whatever you choose to wear when you work magic is up to you.

Just try to find something that helps put you in the right frame of mind and something in which you can work safely. For example, if you're going to be doing a lot of fire dancing I'd avoid long, flowing, flimsy fabrics that can easily catch fire just from exposure to a few sparks. The old saying "safety first" applies in magic, too.

Crystals, Metals, and Minerals
There is little, if anything, on this planet that hasn't been used in the Craft. Crystals, metals, minerals, shells—all of these items and many more appear in instruction books for spells, rituals, charms, and amulets around the world. As with animals, each stone is classified as having specific Elemental correspondences and magical characteristics (often based on the color of the stone or its shape). For example, red stones (the same color as our blood) might be used in magic to treat a blood condition or as energetic talismans.

There's a wide variety of ways to utilize stones in your magic. You can use them to create pendulums, lay them on parts of the body to improve wellness, carry them as portable amulets, add them to spells and rituals as components, visualize them during meditation, plant them to improve the health of your garden, or put them around your sacred space similar to placing candles. The key is to know which crystals are best for whatever purpose you have in mind.

How do you find that out? Well, you can certainly refer to a correspondence list or a book, but I would also recommend that you let the stone speak to you. Each crystal is unique, and it will have certain characteristics that set it apart from every other crystal. The only way to determine those characteristics is to listen with your heart. Hold the stone in your hand, meditate quietly, and see what kinds of feelings or images arise. Take those into account when you use the crystal.

For example, say you're holding quartz, and you feel warm or get the image of a fire in your mind's eye. This implies that the stone has a strong fiery quality, making that quartz similarly energetic. I might then use that stone in a spell to cast the light of truth on a situation or as a charm for physical energy.

Cup or Goblet

Another Goddess symbol, a cup (sometimes a bowl), often holds offerings for the earth or the Divine (water or milk, for example). Also, at some rituals, the coven may drink from one cup filled with a specially chosen beverage to show their unity of mind and spirit. As part of a ritual to support the overall health of coven members, for example, they might sip orange juice.

Horn

While this may serve in the same capacity as a goblet, it has stronger horned god overtones. Some covens may use a horn to announce the opening of a circle or to call the quarters.

Incense

Incense was used by the ancients to cleanse temples, as offerings to gods and goddesses, as a meditative tool, as a cleanser, and as a symbol of prayers or wishes. With this in mind, a little incense is the perfect tool for changing the vibrations in your magical workroom. However, please ask permission from your family before burning anything in small indoor spaces, both for safety and in case someone might be allergic.

Pantry Incense

A lot of the spices in your kitchen rack make excellent incense, too. All you need is a fire source (self-lighting charcoal in a bed of dirt or sand is a good choice) and a pinch of the desired herb. A bit of anise improves psychic ability, basil decreases stress in the house, cinnamon invokes luck, ginger gives you more energy, and nutmeg aids conscious focus, for example.

Knots

Save bits of string, yarn, or even cloth for knot magic. The simple symbolism of tying and releasing makes a knot an ideal implement for spells, charms, amulets, and talismans. You can bind your wishes or goals inside one or more knots, and when you need that energy most, open the knot to release it.

Mirrors

Witches commonly use mirrors for magic dealing with their self-image or as a divination tool. In the case of the latter, the mirror is specially prepared with black paint to which sacred herbs (and sometimes glitter or crushed crystals) are added. You can get as fancy as you want, but the cost to make a basic version is minimal. There are numerous places on the internet where you can find straightforward instructions. Or find *How to Make and Use a Magick Mirror* by Donald Tyson—it's a good book that covers this topic completely.

Music

All the hustle, bustle, noise, pressures, and responsibilities that eat up your day can often be soothed by some good music. I have several favorite albums I play in the background when I'm working magic. You can find many artists, albums, and playlists dedicated specifically to spellwork online.

Bear in mind that thoughtfully choosing music is just as important as any other component of your efforts. Whatever song or album you play, its words, tones, or overall energies should match your goals. Somehow, I can't see playing metal when working a spell for peace, for example. The two just don't mesh.

Finally, you may wish to wear headphones while listening to your music. This closes out the external world and helps you focus your attention on the magic. On a more mundane level, it's a thoughtful gesture that can keep you from getting in trouble for playing music too loudly at home or school.

Plants

The history of witchcraft is closely tied to the folklore and superstitions surrounding the plant kingdom. In prevalent beliefs, some plants aided the witch with their energies. Others kept away unwanted spells, some appeared on altars to Gods and Goddesses, and others still were observed in order to read natural omens and signs. In other words, plants participated in nearly every magical method and mode, and each plant was assigned specific characteristics that witches counted upon in their Craft.

And what of today? Well, here is a brief list of how you can utilize various items from the plant kingdom in your art:

- Put Elementally significant plants around the sacred space so the energy is vital and growing. For example, put a fern in the North, a mint or dandelion plant in the East, chrysanthemums in the South, and a daffodil in the West.

- Choose the flower from a plant that represents a question you have, then tie it into a string and use it as a pendulum. For example, a rosebud might be used to determine questions of love.
- Look up the meaning of various plants that appear in your dreams and use that information to help you interpret those images more accurately.
- Bundle symbolically significant plants together into a power pouch or as part of a charm.
- Bury a plant part to likewise put that type of energy away from you (or help it grow!).
- Release plant matter to flowing water or winds to carry your wishes and energy out to the world.

By the way, the uniqueness I mentioned among crystals works the same way for plants. If you grow anything yourself, you can observe the amount of sunlight, rain, and other conditions that may affect the plant's overall vibrations. Those shifts, in turn, change the way you use the plant in your magic. Using dandelion as an example, this flower bears a signature that helps with divination efforts. One grown in a very wet environment, then, might well be dried and used as part of a divinatory incense for seeing clearly in emotionally charged situations.

Timing
While not a necessary component of your magic, this element has been utilized by a great number of witches over the centuries, and we should pause here to ponder its importance. If we think for a moment of the phrase "as above, so below," it becomes clear that the ancients looked to the stars, Sun, and Moon as important symbols. As the stars changed and the Moon's phases shifted, people naturally believed that the energies also trans-

formed. Wanting to support their magic as much as possible, they looked to astrology to provide them with information as to what energies were being generated by each phase, Moon sign, and Sun sign.

Even today, many spell and ritual books specify the best time for casting magic so that everything above the earth supports the goal. If you would like to try this yourself and gauge the different results, here are some correspondence lists to which you can refer:

Sun Sign Energies
- **Aries:** physical strength, heroism, adventure
- **Taurus:** endurance, dedication
- **Gemini:** diversity, social interaction, humor
- **Cancer:** harmony at home, creativity
- **Leo:** courage, communication
- **Virgo:** logic, reasoning, schooling
- **Libra:** balance, peace
- **Scorpio:** inventiveness, fortitude
- **Sagittarius:** improved energy, abundance
- **Capricorn:** preparation, focus
- **Aquarius:** fresh ideas, fun, crafts
- **Pisces:** kindness, adaptability, dreams

Moon Sign Energies
- **Aries:** cleansing, victory, personal growth
- **Taurus:** devotion, strength, abundance
- **Gemini:** easing into changes, balance
- **Cancer:** creativity, improved money, Moon magic
- **Leo:** developing new skills or talents, Sun magic
- **Virgo:** prosperity, success, strength
- **Libra:** symmetry, seeing the truth, Air magic
- **Scorpio:** self-awareness (especially physical), focused studies

- **Sagittarius:** reaching goals, putting down roots, Fire magic
- **Capricorn:** personal development (internal), Earth magic
- **Aquarius:** playfulness, social interaction, freedom
- **Pisces:** psychic skills, divination, momentum, Water magic

Moon Phase Energies
- **Waxing:** growth-oriented, increase, the Maiden/Son
- **Full:** wisdom, completion, harvest, the Mother/Father
- **Waning:** decrease, banishing, the Crone/Grandfather
- **Dark:** rest, weeding out old habits
- **Blue:** miracles

Now, I'm sure some of you are sitting there saying, "what if a spell or ritual can't wait until the time is just right?" Enact it anyway! Being an effective witch means that you also learn to live and think "out of the box." There are no Ten Commandments here, no absolute requirements. Anytime is the right time for magic if you have the right focus, will, and intention. While there is certainly a time and a place for planning, there are also many things in life that require us to fly by the seat of our broomsticks and just trust.

Magical Etiquette
Since it's likely that you will begin to meet others already practicing or interested in the Craft, it's good to have a feel for some of the general codes of conduct. While these are certainly not carved in stone, a general familiarity with them is a great way to avoid misunderstandings from the get-go.

First, not everyone likes to have their magical tools randomly handled. Before picking up something to look at it, ask the owner if it's okay. Most often, the answer is yes, but if the owner says no, it's for a good reason. If you're curious as to the whys, ask that individual respectfully about how and why that tool is kept apart.

Second, while the Neo-Pagan community is typically very hug-oriented, it is perfectly acceptable to shake hands if you're not a touchy-feely person. Be aware that there are many folks who prefer not to hug. Some even have taboos about personal contact due to their path. When I meet someone new, I typically offer my hand first and see what happens. Also, if you're a minor, it's good to let people know so there's no chance of getting into trouble over age-oriented issues.

Third, you're going to meet a lot of very intelligent folks who enjoy talking about spiritual ideas. As you enter these discussions, ask questions and listen a lot. If you don't know something or don't understand terms, say so. On the other hand, sometimes even the best-intentioned discussion gets dogmatic. If you find yourself swimming in the muck and mire of what's rapidly becoming an "I'm right, you're wrong" type of argument, you can simply excuse yourself, especially since there are many, many magical paths. There's no need to get involved in such battles unless it's a personal ethical issue for which you feel you need to take a stand.

Speaking of taking a stand, if you're ever at a circle and start feeling uncomfortable, it's quite acceptable to bow out. If people are holding hands, I will typically take the two people closest to me and join their hands, then back away. If people aren't holding hands, I slowly walk backward so as to not disrupt things. I think it's very important that you trust yourself to know where you should be and where you should not. After the circle ends, you can go up to the group leader and privately share your reasons for leaving. If that person gives you any flack, this is probably not a good group with whom to continue working.

Along the same lines, if you're near a ritual but not participating, please be thoughtful. Don't talk loudly, play music without headphones, or rummage through your stuff. This is very distracting, not to mention inconsiderate of those people who are trying to raise energy. This ties into what I call "observer" etiquette. For example, imagine that you are observing someone who is obviously meditating. Unless it's an emergency, this isn't the time to tap them on the shoulder and ask for something.

Finally, if you're at a gathering, do not take pictures of anyone without permission. Not everyone in our community can come out of the broom closet yet. If such pictures land in the wrong hands, people can lose jobs, among other things. If you follow these basic guidelines and add your own common sense, your magical interactions will flow a lot more smoothly.

Getting It All Together
When I discovered that other people saw the world similarly, it was a great relief. Before that moment I had felt very alone, and I'd begun losing hope that I would ever find the kind of kinship I was seeking. Now that I have, there are certainly still many days when I feel like I'll never get it all together. Nonetheless, being a witch is very comfortable to me and I know I'm exactly where I should be. But just because it's right for me doesn't mean it must be right for you.

If I could ask you to do one favor for me while you read, it would be to remember this point. My wish for you is that you find something that sings the song of your heart and spirit (not mine). I can only be here on paper, and there are a lot of questions or situations that a book of this size simply cannot cover. Therefore, I have to trust that you'll start listening to your inner voice and following your vision with confidence.

Say, for example, if part of what I've shared thus far (and in the rest of this book) feels right, and part of it does not—that's really okay! In putting together your spiritual path, it's perfectly acceptable to take the best things you find from several different sources and respectfully blend them into something that works for you. In fact, it's what I recommend doing because it requires thoughtfulness and also results in something far more meaningful to you.

From this moment forward, you are in the driver's seat for the way you handle your spirituality. Quite honestly you were there all along, but circumstances never gave you access to the keys! Being a witch is one of those keys, but you're the only person with access to the "ignition" in your soul. Stop. Breathe deeply and think one more time about whether this is right for you. If it is—turn the key and the page and we'll start together!

Chapter IV

Come *Sit* for a *Spell*: Locker Charms and Backpack Blessings

Spellcraft is one of the key methods in all magic and one in which most people are eager to learn more. Note, however, that the spells you'll see here will not "turn Johnny into a toad" or "make Suzy love me." There are a lot of reasons for this, not the least of which are ethical considerations. As witches, we should focus on the positives. The idea is to be proactive, to make our lives happier and better, and by extension, improve the world. Revenge, anger, bitterness, and other similar emotions, when acted upon spiritually, certainly don't help achieve that goal. In fact, they undermine it.

I want to focus most of our time on providing you with ideas about creating and adapting spells according to your personal daily needs and goals. This is very similar to the old saying, "give a man a fish, you feed him for a day. Teach him to fish, and you feed him for a lifetime." While you can find tons of spells in dozens of books (and a few here, too), ultimately, learning the "how to" of spellcraft is what feeds your magical aptitude for a lifetime!

Fundamental Spellcraft

There are two key principles to spellcraft that, if you learn them now, will help you greatly in your efforts. The first is the Law of Sympathy. This means that any symbolic item, when used correctly, becomes what it represents or acts upon what it represents in the spiritual sense. I know that sounds a little weird, so let me give you an example. If we choose to use a poppet (a doll) to represent a sick friend and then direct a healing spell into that poppet, the energy acts upon our friend, not upon the doll. Similarly, if you come across an old spell that calls for something unsafe or unethical (like blood), you can substitute red juice for that component and not lose any meaning, symbolism, or power.

The second principle is the Law of Similarity. While these two tie together, they're slightly different. In this case, the patterns in nature are trusted to give us clues as to how to best utilize the earth's storehouse. For example, if you find a heart-shaped stone, that might well be used as part of a relationship charm or amulet because the shape implies its function. Another example is the poppet we discussed previously. If your friend had a chill and you wrapped the doll in a soft, warm cloth as part of your spell, you're showing the universe the desired effect of your magic! The actions and chosen accoutrements shape your energy, just like the shape of the stone indicates a good potential application for it.

As you read over more spells, you'll see these two principles illustrated again and again, which will help you understand them better. Oh, and if you're feeling nervous about the idea of constructing or adapting spells, relax. Magic is a birthright. Yes, it takes practice to become really adept at it, just like it takes practice to be a professional soccer player or gymnast. Everybody has to start somewhere!

Ethics of Spellcraft

The Laws of Sympathy and Similarity provide the black-and-white outlines that begin to express why the witch designs spells a specific way and a theory of why they work, but that's really only the beginning. Within that framework, you've got a lot of room for individualization. One thing that there's not a lot of room for, however, is the unethical application of power.

You've probably heard this before, but it's always good to remind ourselves of sound spiritual ethics before we begin creating, adapting, or casting spells. Neo-Wiccans should strive to work their magic for the greatest good (the Good of All). The rule of "harm none" applies to yourself, others, animals, the planet, and by extension all things in the universe.

I'll be the first to admit that it's tempting sometimes to cast a spell in anger or sadness (or other dark places of the mind and heart), but I can also tell you it won't satisfy you. I remember enacting such a spell once, and I honestly didn't like the person I saw in myself that day. From that moment forward, I promised the only time I would use magic as a weapon is when I or someone I love has been purposefully harmed (and I know from where that harm comes). Even then, I only use magic when mundane efforts to rectify things fail.

Having said all that, I'm not your magical "sitter." I won't be there when you create or cast spells. Rather I have to trust that each person reading this has the maturity to accept the responsibility that goes with what they're about to do—for good or ill, it's all in your lap. You're not a little kid who doesn't know right from wrong. You're a young adult, and I'm speaking to you the same way I would speak to any adult student before they undertake spellcraft.

What exactly do I tell my students about ethics? Simply, be thoughtful. Think about the potential outcomes of your magic and how they may affect people or situations. Think about your motivations and overall mood. Take a deep breath and just pause for a moment; perform a self-check. Are you sure it's for the greatest good (or just what you think is good)? And most important, will you like and respect the person looking back from your mirror after this spell is done? Most often, if you take just a moment for this check-up, you'll rarely make the wrong choice.

Basic Spell Types

Note: You may wish to set up your Book of Shadows with these subheadings for your spells for quick reference.

- **Physical Spells:** Those that require only one's body to enact, such as what the people of the Middle Ages called the "evil eye" or the hand-motion blessing of a Priest/ess. Physical spells were typically used for banishing, charming, and healing.
- **Verbal Spells:** Often called "charms," these need nothing more than your words to direct the energy. Most verbal spells rhyme (it makes them easier to remember). The word *charm* also means "song," and there's no reason you could not sing your spells if you like! Historically, charms were often used to attract love, encourage luck, and safeguard health.
- **Written Spells:** Another very common medium. Words have power, and the pattern of words, the medium they are written upon, and the aroma of the ink all

shape that power into a specific intention. Written spells are commonly used in healing arts and as part of wishes.

- **Component Spells:** Candles, knots, herbs, crystals—all the tools in a witch's kit may become components and focal points in his or her art. Component-oriented spells are among the most widely seen, in part because they offer the greatest variety of potential applications.
- **Visualized Spells:** Typically combined with a meditative process, everything having to do with this type of spell is created in the mind's eye and carried out on the mind's stage. A simple example is the white-light bubble visualization many people use to cast a protective sphere around themselves.
- **Elemental Spells:** Similar to component spells, these utilize a specific Elemental component (Soil, Wind, Water, Fire) as a means of empowering the spell or giving it greater focus. For example, taking a written wish and floating it on water moving away from you falls under this category because the water bears your emotions, your wish is directed outward. Burning that very same paper releases the wish to Spirit, where the winds disperse it by smoke. Planting it helps the wish to grow, and so forth.

Adapting Spells

When you begin practicing magic, it's often easier to work with spells that have been designed by witches with a little more experience than you have. It's not absolutely necessary, but most folks feel more comfortable in taking this route. Better still, working through prefabricated spells gives you a feel for what you like, what you don't, and what works for you (along with the whole spell-crafting process). That's how I learned to create my own spells, and I think you might find it works for you too.

Most prefabricated spells are "proofed" before going into a book to make sure the process runs smoothly and the results seem sound. Nonetheless, not all of these spells are going to feel right to you simply because the creator of the magic is not you! See, I can write spells that I know work for me because I understand the symbols and actions to which I relate best—which ones inspire me, hone my will, and guide my focus. But every person is unique, and your spiritual perspectives will likewise be unique.

So, as you read the spells I provide, or those in any other book, ask yourself:

- Do the spell's components make sense to me?
- Does this wording make me uncomfortable, or are the words something I wouldn't normally use in daily speech?
- Does the spell include words in any foreign languages (and if so, do you understand the meanings of those words in that language)?
- Do I understand the spell's terminology completely?
- Does the spell seem to direct its energy toward my specific goal or need?
- Is there any action prescribed here that makes me uncomfortable or seems out of place?
- Are there any components I cannot use due to circumstances (like a burning candle if your parents don't allow open flame)?
- Does the spell seem manipulative or negative in any way?

If you answered yes to any of those questions, but you like the overall construction of the spell, that's where the adaptation process begins. Go through the spell one step at a time. Change any words, actions, or components you feel necessary to make this process truly meaningful and wholly representative of your goal. Try to keep it simple. No one ever said magic had to be fancy to be effective (meaning no shades of Shakespeare need appear in your words).

The only guideline you must follow for success is that your substitutions should maintain the symbolic value. For example, if the spell you have calls for burning lavender (a common ingredient in spells for peace, harmony, and sleep) and you're allergic to lavender, you'll want to find another herb with similar properties. One option here would be chamomile (which is also used for peace and sleep). Continue in this manner with each point of the spell, gather what you need, and you're good to go!

Now, some of you might be wondering what spell books you should review to find potential spells for adaptation. That's not an easy question, because there are so many magical books that include a variety of spells. However, there are some good guidelines you can use in making your choice:

- Does the spell's creator promise 100% results every time? (If so, warning bells should go off—no one can ethically make that claim.)
- Do you respect the author of the spell and the way they communicate? If not, you're probably not going to respect or relate well to that approach to spellcraft either.
- Has a trusted friend or family member recommended that book or author to you? If not, have you checked for reviews of the book online?

Following these three points will typically keep you away from spells and/or writers that are not right for you.

Creating New Spells

Once you know how to adapt spells, you'll find making your own much easier. The only difference is that you have a lot more to think about because you're designing the construct from scratch. Every point—the timing, the symbols, the actions, the words—all come from you. The steps provided here will help you put everything together in a logical manner. No, don't let the word logic put you off here—we use our rational mind's responses to help us choose the best possible ingredients for the magic we're cooking up.

Here's the step-by-step process for designing your own spells:

1. Ask yourself what your goal is. Find a few words that describe that purpose and write them down.
2. Pick out one of the basic spell types (or a combination) that you'd like to use (i.e., physical, verbal, written, component, visualized, or Elemental). Remember that the goal of the spell should be reflected in this choice. For example, I would not consider using a verbal spell to halt gossip. The goal of such a spell is "quieting" words, not creating them.
3. Returning to the key themes you noted in step one, consider what components you have available that have those energies and will work harmoniously with your chosen spell type. For example, perhaps you want to use a yellow candle for a communication spell, but this would be difficult if you're using the Element of Water to carry the energy. The only way you might combine these two is by finding a floating candle rather than a standard taper.

4. Also, consider what items you have in or around the house that symbolize or support your goal. For example, if you're having trouble concentrating in one of your classes, some of the things that might make ideal components include a notebook, a special pen, or even a book that you use in that class (to which you could add a specially designed cover energized by your spell).
5. Consider using special timing for the spell (refer to Chapter Three for ideas). This is an optional step.
6. Does your spell require any physical actions to emphasize its goal? This is typically true in any "physical spell" but also may be true in others. For example, if you're directing magic toward a person or part of the world, pointing that way makes sense (in this case, your finger becomes a wand).
7. Cleanse, bless, and/or charge all the components of your spell to eliminate any unwanted energies and activate the components' potential. If you're not familiar with these processes, they're not difficult. Cleansing alleviates random energy from an item. To cleanse it, you can wash the item in spring water with a bit of salt or lemon juice or pass it through the smoke of a purifying incense like cedar or frankincense.
8. Charging isn't very difficult. Think of it like using a battery to energize your work, but with spiritual symbolism. Many witches use the light of the Sun or Moon as the "batteries" to charge objects (sunlight for conscious, logical, and mundane matters and moonlight for intuitive, spiritual, and subconscious work). Just place the item in the chosen light for several minutes or hours so it absorbs that energy.

9. Lastly, blessing is a way to ask for Divine assistance and designate each item for its purpose in the spell. Traditionally, a blessing consists of laying one's hand on the item and verbally or mentally praying for blessings. Returning to our example of the candle, you might hold it in one hand and say, "God/dess bless this candle that is about to represent open and honest communications in my magic."
10. Design the spell. Now it's time to get down to brass tacks. It's time to figure out how you want all your symbols to go together in the spell itself. With our communication candle, you might want to carve it with a symbol, then dab it with oil before lighting it, for example. As you light the candle, that would be a good time for an incantation (a verbal expression of your will).
11. Last, how long the candle burns can also be symbolic, like leaving it for eight minutes for authoritative speech, or an hour for cooperative discussions.
12. Create sacred space. Another optional step, but a good one. This helps keep your energy firmly in place until you're ready to release it toward the goal. Chapter Two offers a brief example of creating sacred space, and there are more details and examples in Chapter Seven.
13. Cast the spell! Now, all that remains to be done is to give your process a try. Remember to keep your mind focused on your goal and your will sure from beginning to end. As you work through it, make a mental note of anything that doesn't feel quite right, like words over which you stumble. You

can use this information in tailoring spells in the future or adapting this one so it flows more easily!
14. Make notes of your experience in a magical diary. You may want to refer to this later, especially to gauge results.
15. Watch for manifestation. Those spells that manifest effectively are good ones to put in your Book of Shadows.

Expectations

A lot of people ask me what kind of results they can expect from any spell. The answer to that question depends a lot on:

- How well the spell was constructed
- How much emotional and mental connection the caster has to the components and process
- How well the spell's words and components delineate the goal
- How much focus and will the individual put into the spell
- Whether or not the spell was completed without interruptions
- Whether or not the phrase "for the greatest good" or something similar was included in the spell

As mentioned previously, even the most soundly constructed spell may not work for you if you don't understand all the parts, or if they hold no personal meaning. Since manifestation is driven by your focus and will, if you should lose your concentration, you'll get some iffy results at best. And, if you've asked the universe to step in and guide the energy for the good of all, the way your spell manifests could be quite surprising.

Let me share just one of my favorite stories with you that illustrates some of these points. There was a young woman who cast a fine spell to find a companion. Her will and focus was sure, and the spell included the universal clause so as to not interfere with free will. Then one day her perfect companion appeared, with the right hair color, eye color, and personality. It was a dog. So, what happened here? Well, she never indicated she wanted a human companion (it's often in the details—the Universe has a sense of humor). She also asked that the spell work for the greatest good, which in this case seemed to be having a companion that loves unconditionally. In this case, the dog became a great companion!

Precautions

We've already talked about avoiding magic when you're ill, angry, or otherwise out of sorts. Are there any other things about which you should be cautious other than those listed earlier this chapter? Yes, a few. For one thing, never use an herb or plant with which you're unfamiliar. Also, if you don't know if you might be allergic to a food, beverage, or herb presented as an edible spell (like some of the potions and munchies in this chapter), do not use it. Find a substitute. This is very important since magic is intended to help you, not hurt you (harm none applies to you, too!) and allergic reactions are certainly no fun and potentially dangerous.

Along the same lines, be considerate of the people in your living space. If a spell calls for the dabbing of an aromatic oil or burning incense that might irritate an allergy they have, find a substitute. Finally, try not to use up the last bit of an herb, food, or beverage (or anything else) in the house just for a spell. While the spell might go off without a hitch, I'm willing to bet that your folks or housemates won't be amused by the missing item(s). When in doubt, ask first!

With those precautions aside, here are some spells to try, adapt, put in your Book of Shadows, or use as a pattern for your own.

Anger on Ice

A friend's been rude, your parents seem unfair, all hell is breaking loose at school, and for whatever reason you're feeling really pissy. Anger has a tendency to skew magic, not to mention our mundane ability to focus and handle things effectively. So, how do you cool off quickly?

Besides taking several deep breaths, take a piece of paper and write the reason for your anger on it. Let everything come out. Write as long as you need to get it all down and out of your system. Now, fold this paper in thirds, saying:

> *"Calm in mind,*
> *Calm in mind and body,*
> *Calm in mind, body, and spirit."*

Put the paper into a dish that holds enough water to cover it and put it in the freezer to literally cool down the negative energy. Leave it there until the situation is resolved.

An alternative way of helping alleviate anger is by making yourself an enchanted potion of one part apple juice and one part peach or passion fruit juice (both of which encourage peace). First, stir the blend counterclockwise (to decrease negativity), saying:

> *"Dispel the anger, dispel all doubt.*
> *It's time for me to just chill out!"*

Then stir clockwise, saying:

> *"I am focused, cool, and calm,*
> *This potion acts like a healing balm."*

Drink the beverage before you go back into the situation that brought about the anger. This spell will help to keep you centered and in control of your emotions.

Banish the Blues

Age doesn't matter—everyone gets sad and depressed sometimes. It might be in response to an unhappy event, or it could just be part of a mental or physical cycle, but no matter the cause it's no fun. It's even worse when you feel like you can't do anything to change how you feel. But you can! And here's one way to do it.

For this spell, you're going to need a handful of marigold petals, oregano, or lettuce. If using the lettuce, gently tear it into small sections like you might for a salad. All three of these plants symbolize joy, happiness, and contentment. Take them outside at dawn if possible (the time of renewed hope) or just before you go to school. Sprinkle them on the ground in a clockwise circle just as the first rays of the Sun reach you (sunshine represents blessings). As you release them, speak your wish, using something like this:

> *"Depression released;*
> *negativity ceased, sadness be gone,*
> *burned away in the hope of dawn.*

*The light of a new day,
brings all good things my way."*

Stand there for a few minutes until some of the flower, herb, or lettuce has been moved by the wind (this represents your wish's energy moving outward toward manifestation). Absorb a little of that warm sunlight and hold it close throughout the day. Repeat as necessary until you feel better.

An alternative here would be to pick out your favorite comfort food or drink and take it outside at dawn or before school. In this case, I'd suggest holding the cup up to the Sun (so it absorbs that energy) while speaking the incantation. Just change it a little to reflect your new medium, like this:

*"Depression released;
negativity ceased, sadness be gone,
burned away in the hope of dawn.
The light of a new day,
brings all good things my way.
This potion when taken within, the spell begins!"*

Drink the beverage down completely to fully accept the energy into yourself.

Class Communication

My son hates class presentations. As he puts it, they give him "vultures" in his stomach. Even the old trick of staring at one point at the back of the room doesn't seem to help. If you have similar problems, try this spell to improve your communication skills for class:

You'll need a small container of honey (something the size of a lip gloss vial is fine) and a piece of yellow construction paper. Write the topic of your talk on the yellow paper. Wrap the container of honey with that paper (yellow is the color that supports communicative skills). Since communication in this setting stresses the conscious mind, put this bundle in the light of the sun for about three minutes (three's a charm, and it encourages overall luck, which you can use). The whole time it sits in the sunshine, repeat an incantation like:

> *"When this honey I take and taste,*
> *Words be sure, fears abate,*
> *Help me to communicate.*
> *When I stand before my class,*
> *By this spell, my fears are past!"*

Take this with you to school and put a little honey on your tongue before you give your presentation or talk. For those who may be allergic to honey, anything minty will do just as well. Both mint and honey are associated with our ability to relate ideas in the best possible way. Honey is also associated with creativity.

Creativity's Cooking

Speaking of creativity, I'm sure there are a lot of homework assignments and other projects or problems that come up in your life that require a bit of ingenuity. This spell is intended to generate that kind of energy. It begins with an image of a tortoise (these creatures represent slow, steady progress, inventiveness, and long-lasting stability, all of which combine nicely to support your goal). Look at that picture for a while until you can see it clearly in your mind, then close your eyes.

Imagine the tortoise's outline as brilliant sparkling white and golden light. Shrink that portrait down so you can reach out in the visualization, grab it, and place it on your third eye (between your eyebrows). Let the light image absorb into your energetic body. To this process you might want to add an affirmation that you repeat four times each (the number of completion). Example affirmations for this goal include:

> *"I am creative.*
> *I am insightful.*
> *I am successful.*
> *I am imaginative."*

When you go into the project or problem in question, repeat this affirmation four times again to reinforce the energy in and around you.

Doubt Deterrent

Every day each of us makes dozens of decisions—what to wear, what to eat for breakfast, how much time to study, and so on. Some decisions are pretty easy, while others leave us with nagging doubts about what's best. Then, of course, there are all those odd little situations that come up in daily life that leave you wondering about what's true and how you should respond. This can become very frustrating. When you're finding that doubt is keeping you from acting or thinking clearly, try this spell.

Get some thyme (the fresher, the better; if it's organic, that would be best, as this yields a purer aromatic oil).

However, if you only have the dried herb at home, that will work. On the night of a waning moon (so troubles shrink), take a pinch in your hand and crush it (if you need to use a mortar and pestle, do so). As you crush the herb, say:

> *"Doubt crushed,*
> *Doubt hushed,*
> *No more to be torn,*
> *Right here, certainty is born!"*

Take a little of the fresh oils generated from the herb and dab it on your heart chakra and both wrists. This provides courage and assurance. Also, package up a little of this oil and take it with you. That way, if you feel yourself slipping, you can just repeat the incantation and apply some fresh oil.

Gossip Stopper

Gossip comes from people with way too much time on their hands. Whether it's driven by jealousy or just misinformation, it's typically hurtful and destructive. Whenever you're faced with gossip, I suggest two things—first, go directly to the source and ask. A lot of times you can nip rumors in the bud just by daring to be different and getting to the truth. If that doesn't work to improve matters, then try this spell.

You'll need some lipstick and a piece of paper. Black paper might be a good choice since you want to banish the gossip. Draw a pair of lips on the paper using the lipstick, saying:

*"Close the lips that lie,
The truth shall be known by and by,
All gossip that's harmful and running the mill
By my will—those tongues be stilled!"*

Now fold the paper in half so that the top lip touches the bottom one. Clip, staple, or clothespin this in place and keep it somewhere safe until the rumors pass.

Gorgeous Glamour

There are times when we all want to look and feel our best. Glamour is a spell designed to help with just that, by creating a specific type of atmosphere around you. In this case, you wrap yourself in an atmosphere that people perceive as being more attractive and self-assured. While you can do this through simple visualization, I know a lot of people who have trouble with that particular practice. So, I recommend making a glamour oil instead.

To be attractive to young men, you'll need about half a cup of good virgin olive oil or almond oil and about seven drops each of any of the following (or a blend): neroli, musk, lavender, gardenia, ginger, or jasmine. To be attractive to young women, use the same proportions but focus on additives like bay, patchouli, vetiver, violet, or civet. If you want to appeal to a wide variety of people, try mixing one or two aromatics from both lists.

You'll want to keep the oil in a dark, airtight bottle. Place it in the light of a full moon to energize it for about three hours (the number of body, mind, and spirit working together). Dab it on just before going into a public or private situation with the person or persons whose attention you hope to gain. Begin at your heart (so that you work in perfect love), saying:

> *"Let the best of me shine,*
> *in your heart and mine."*
> *[Move to the third eye chakra.]*
> *"See with your inner eye*
> *where my attributes lie."*
> *[Move to dab some on your hands.]*
> *"My hand is open to friendship,"*
> *[Move to your ears.]*
> *"my ears to the truth,"*
> *[Move back to your heart.]*
> *"and my heart to love."*

Make sure to store your oil in a cool area. If it begins to look cloudy, that means the oil has begun to turn and you'll have to make a new batch. Once the oil spoils, so does the magic it contained.

Homeroom Health

Everyone around you coming down with colds and flu? Have a big date, prom, or other important social function coming up and want to stay healthy? Well, first do all the normal things—take your vitamins, drink lots of fluids, and keep out of drafts and damp weather. It never hurts to be cautious! Second, whip yourself up a batch of healthy magic.

For this, I suggest using orange juice in a silver-toned cup. The juice naturally bolsters your immune system and represents health, while the silver cup adds a protective element. Consider enacting this spell near an open window when the sun is shining (fresh air and sunshine are healthy). Place your strong hand palm down over the cup. Visualize a bright white light pouring into it as you say:

> *"Heed my words, empower my spell,*
> *Through this potion keep me well!"*

Drink the juice afterward. You can do this every day until the people around you are healthier. By the way, there's no reason why you can't put some of this juice into a thermos or other container to have for lunch. This way, you internalize your magic throughout the day.

Lady Luck

A little bit of luck makes a lot of things easier and more pleasant. When you feel as if good fortune keeps missing you, try increasing your chances to benefit from it with this little spell, which starts with an apple. Slice your apple horizontally in about quarter-inch slices so you can see the pentagram formed by the seed pattern in the center. Lay these out on a cookie cooling rack.

Next, take some warm water in which you've placed a personally lucky number of allspice berries, a pinch of basil, and a few breadcrumbs. Stir this clockwise with your finger, saying:

> *"In this water my magic I bind,*
> *Lady luck be good, gentle, and kind."*

Using the same finger, dab the five points of the pentagram visible on each apple slice with the water starting at the East, saying:

> *"By the Power of Wind, I invoke luck,*
> *By the Power of Fire, I invite good fortune,*
> *By the Power of Water, I welcome blessings,*
> *By the Power of Earth, opportunities grow,*
> *By Spirit—all are bound together with my will.*
> *So be it!"*

Finally, cover the slices with a loose-weave cloth, leaving them to air dry completely. Hang them decoratively in any area to which you want to bring more luck regularly.

Relationship Rescue

When a friendship or more serious relationship hits a rocky place it not only affects you but often everyone around you. If you feel like your personal efforts to fix things have gone unnoticed, awry, or completely blown up in your face, try this spell.

First, find one candle in your favorite color and dab it with a bit of your personal perfume or cologne. Alternatively, carve your name into it. Second, take a candle to represent the other person. On this candle, place a scented oil that correlates with their birth sign as follows:

- **Cancer:** agrimony, sage, or jasmine
- **Leo:** sage or marigold
- **Virgo:** cedar, orange, lemon, or cinnamon
- **Libra:** bergamot, basil, or geranium
- **Scorpio:** basil, rose, or patchouli

- **Sagittarius:** dandelion, sandalwood, or hyssop
- **Capricorn:** comfrey, cedar, or bay
- **Aquarius:** anise or wisteria
- **Pisces:** rose or jasmine
- **Aries:** bay, cinnamon, or orange
- **Taurus:** orange, grapefruit, or jasmine
- **Gemini:** mint or rosemary

By the way, if oil isn't handy, you can rub dried herb on the candle—moving from the bottom to the top to increase positive energy.

Next, find a fire-safe container in which to put the candles and a place to put them in your room that's away from curtains and other flammable items (no need to ignite the only place in the house that's really yours). Each morning for one week, light your candle and then use it to light the other candle. When you put your candle down, move it a little closer toward the other until they finally meet on the Sunday of that week. At that time, the two candles get blown out simultaneously, bound together in red and white ribbon, and kept safe so that the relationship also stays "safe." If the two of you ever go your separate ways, these candles should be burned completely (in separate containers) so any anger and pain is burned away and stays in the past.

Wishing Well

Neither adapted nor personally created spells have to be overly complicated to work. In fact, many of our traditional wishing customs are mini spells that, when blended with magical focus and will, work just fine. Toss a coin in a well or fountain while speaking your desire to the winds. Whisper your needs to the first star appearing.

It's all a kind of magic, and you have the power within to make those wishes come true.

My favorite wishing spell is very simple. You'll need an empty jar. Every day when you come home, put your spare change in the jar and make a wish. It helps if you focus on just one wish at a time for greater manifesting power. When the jar is full, give away the contents to a good cause. This in turn brings that gift back to you three-fold (by the Law of Three and Law of Sympathy).

Taking it on the Road

Teens today are as mobile as their parents, if not more so. That means you need easily transportable charms, amulets, and talismans that are made from everyday items. This section provides information on how to make such items out of easily obtainable components, empower them, and then utilize them for daily needs.

Rather than put the cart before the horse, I'd like to explain the difference between these three types of "pocket magic" because the basic terminology is often confused or misused. (I call it "pocket magic" because you can literally put the resulting token in your pocket and take it with you wherever you go). Let's start with charms, which were among the very first types of spells ever devised, if not *the* first.

The original form of a charm was simply a set of words that rhymed, sometimes being sung. The beauty of the charm is that you need nothing more than your voice (or your thoughts) to create the desired energy. Why thoughts? Well, there are times when you can't just begin chanting or reciting the spell out loud, and our thoughts are simply internal conversations. They are every bit as powerful as the spoken word, so long as your focus and will are honed.

Now, what about the small tokens we call charms? That was a later development, likely intended to add symbolic value. But whether contrived as an object or a set of words, the major purpose for a charm was that of encouraging luck, love, and overall well-being (including safety).

Charms are considered an elementary magic. They're designed to release their energy slowly, kind of like a timed-release spiritual vitamin. This means you may have to repeat the words or recharge the item periodically to keep the energy moving forward.

Next, we come to amulets. This is where things get a little confusing. The word *amulet* means "to make a charm," so clearly charms and amulets are related. In reviewing traditional amulets, two things seem to set them apart. For one, amulets always have a component (like a stone or a ring). For another, amulets were intended to protect the bearer or remedy sickness. Additionally, the instructions for amulet making are often very precise, each step of the preparation appears to be essential to positive results.

Amulets don't lose their energy as quickly as charms. Rather, they remain turned "off" until a situation calls that energy into action. For example, a protective amulet would be switched on by an impending automobile accident. Thanks to this passive nature, amulets last a long time unless their attributes are repeatedly and regularly necessary to the bearer. I find this is sometimes true with folks who live in highly urbanized areas. Because there are more people, and more surrounding negative energies, the amulet tends to discharge faster.

Finally, we come to talismans. Where the amulet was passive, talismans are active. This means that like a charm you may need to re-energize a talisman or create one for a "disposable" purpose (like carrying one for a while then burning or burying it to remove specific energy from your life). Additionally, like a charm, part of the process of making a talisman is the use of an incantation (verbal component) to create the desired indwelling energy. Conversely, the main thing that sets talismans apart from the other two types of pocket magic is the fact that they are traditionally made during auspicious astrological times.

Here are some sample charms, amulets, and talismans for you to try, adapt, or use as prototypes in making your own.

Confidence Charm
For most people, confidence is tied to self-image. That's why this charm combines a small, palm-size mirror with affirmations. To prepare the mirror, take a drop of mint flavoring, fennel water (or marjoram), and some onion juice, and blend them together. You don't need a lot and feel free to go light on the onion juice so the aroma isn't overly strong. These three ingredients bear the energies for alleviating anxiety, improving courage, and overall clarity of mind and spirit.

Using the index finger of your strong hand, apply this to the outer edge of the mirror moving clockwise, saying:

> *"Mirror, mirror let me see,*
> *All I am and all I can be.*
> *Mirror, Mirror, when to you I speak,*
> *Assurance and resoluteness is what I seek.*
> *Mirror, Mirror, where my magic shines,*
> *By this spell, confidence is mine."*

Next, apply a little glue in the same area where you put the blend. Sprinkle glitter on the glue and let it dry completely. The glitter is purely for a sparkle effect when you look into the surface later when using the mirror, so consider this step optional. Wrap the mirror in a white cloth to keep it from cracking or chipping when carried.

Keep this with you, and the next time you feel your confidence waning, look into it. As you do, repeat affirmations like these several times to release the indwelling magic:

> *"I am self-assured.*
> *I am confident.*
> *I have presence and charisma."*

Note that you can make the affirmations more situation-specific by adding a few more words to the sentence. For example, if you need confidence for a literature exam, you might say, *"I am self-assured in English."* Repeat this phrase silently in your mind when you run across a test question that's leaving you uncertain.

Warning: This charm is not a substitute for good study methods.

Decision Dice
Have you come to a crossroads? Or perhaps there are just too many options from which to choose? You can make a decision die to help you. (Note: This will only work for up to six options.)

Decision-making is a conscious action, but instincts play a role, too. So, wait until the Moon is full and set the die in that light for as long as you wish. The following morning, set it in sunlight for an equal amount of time. This provides balance.

Next, take a little coffee and dab it on all six surfaces. Coffee bears the energy of alertness, clarity, and mindfulness. As you touch the numbers, add this incantation (repeating it one time each for the number on the surface of the die you're touching— in other words, once on the one, twice on the two, and so on):

> *"With the touch of one, this spell is begun.*
> *With the touch of two, my magic's true.*
> *With the touch of three, the power is freed.*
> *With the touch of four, I open the door.*
> *With the touch of five, this spell's alive.*
> *With the touch of six, a decision is fixed!"*

Keep this die with you. When you find yourself facing a difficult choice, take it out and hold it in your hand. Think of the decision ahead and all the options with as much clarity as possible. If there are a lot of different options, write them down in order (one to six) beforehand. When you feel the die getting warm, roll it on a flat surface. You can interpret the results in one of two ways. The first way is if you had a specific preferred choice in mind already.

- **One:** Yes. A "go-ahead" signal. Your choice is a good one.
- **Two:** No. Reconsider.
- **Three:** Move ahead cautiously with your plans but realize there may be more going on than you know.
- **Four:** Consider your other options more carefully before making a final move.
- **Five:** Be patient. You need not rush this right now.
- **Six:** You already know what's best in your heart— so do it!

The second way to interpret the number is that it represents the best decision from your list of options. In either case, don't let yourself be wholly dependent on this amulet—listen to the witch within!

Dream and Sleep Sachet
There is nothing worse than counting the dots on ceiling tiles or fibers in the carpet when all you want to do is sleep. You're not the first to face this problem. Old magical books are filled with nighttime remedies for both restlessness and bad dreams.

One of my favorite items that helps with both concerns is a dream pillow. However, rather than use a lot of herbs and fabric, we're going to assemble something smaller and more portable. This way, you can even take it with you if you wish.

Begin with a small pouch or a 4" x 4" scrap of dark blue or purple fabric (both are dreamy, restful colors). Place a small, tumbled agate and amethyst, a geode, rosemary, sage, thyme, and lavender into this pouch. The agate is protective, the amethyst promotes relaxation, and the geode captures good dreams. The rosemary, sage, and thyme help you remember your dreams, while the lavender supports a restful sleep. If you had a baby blanket as a child, or something similar from which you still have a small scrap, that also makes an excellent component for your sleep sachet; it offers comfort and familiarity. Tie the pouch or bundle securely and bless it, saying something like:

> *"Through this pouch, my magic seeps,*
> *to bring to me a night of sleep.*
> *And dreams that come, be revealing and kind,*
> *remembered tomorrow in my waking mind."*

Place this under your pillow or in a drawer next to the bed for best results.

Heartbreak Healer

Have a friend who's left you out in the cold? A date that dumped you or stood you up? These sorts of circumstances hurt a lot, and generally you don't start feeling better overnight. But magic can become a helpmate in coping.

First, you should know it's really okay to cry! Life isn't always perfect, and tears release pain. Sucking it up because you feel you have to be strong is actually quite harmful, as is stuffing your feelings down deep inside. If you respond in this way, you'll find you get distracted, angrier, confused, and lose your focus.

For what it's worth, my advice is to let yourself feel for a while before trying a magical approach. After you've had a chance to get rid of some of the lingering negativity and can better direct your will, make this amulet to encourage improved spirits and to protect your heart.

You'll need a black marker, a piece of red construction paper, some medicinal ointment (like the kind used on cuts that clean out infection and aid healing), tape, cotton, and some type of small box or jar with a cap. First, cut the paper so it's shaped like your heart. Write the name of the person, group, or situation that caused you pain in the middle. Now, focus whatever is left of your sadness on that paper. Holding one edge in each hand, tear the heart in two (this symbolizes your ability to separate yourself from that negative energy).

Next, take three deep cleansing breaths. Let go of any remaining sadness or pain until you feel empty. Tape the heart back together (to begin the healing process) and put salve on the paper wound (per the Law of Sympathy). Fold this inward on itself until it will fit into the container you've chosen. Inside the container, make a bed of cotton (or use a different material that's soft and comforting) on which to place the heart. Carry this with you until you're feeling like yourself again and can see those people or go into those situations without emotionally falling apart.

Finally, when all is well again, bury the paper or burn it. That pain is gone and in the past. You need not keep the amulet any longer. It's done its job.

Friendship Key

In the scheme of things, friends are treasures. They make you feel better when you're blue, they listen even when you just want to vent, and they always seem to understand what you're saying even when you might not! But it's not always easy to find friends, or at least those who will really be good friends. That's where this little charm comes in.

To make it, all you need is an old key (any will do, but you need to be able to distinguish it from the other ones you may have) and a little lemon juice (fresh or reconstituted). Rub the lemon juice into the key; this is for attracting the right people your way, whereas the key is there to open the doors for conversation. Empower your key by repeating this incantation twice:

*"Open the way; open the way,
Friends to find, by night or day.
Those who will listen, the ones who are sincere,
Those who are fun, from out of my peers.
When I touch this magic key,
By my will this spell be freed!"*

When you're about to go into a situation where you might meet some new folks, touch the key and mentally repeat the incantation to release the magic. Use this only twice, then re-empower it.

Pocket Peer Protection

Every school and neighborhood has at least a few bullies and cliques. Some of these people really haven't figured out yet how to play nicely with others. Avoidance does some good as does having a healthy dose of humor, but when those seem to fail, try reaching into your magic kit for some protective aid.

Obviously, you want this to be something that you can wear or carry all the time. I'd suggest a watch, necklace, ear cuff, nose ring, or even contacts or sunglasses. The last one has the extra symbolic value enabling you to "see" trouble before it sees you!

You want to work with solar energy for this amulet, so let your chosen item charge up in the light of the sun for at least an hour. If it's something that might be damaged by the heat, indirect light will do the trick just fine. Next, you're going to designate this item's task with your incantation—something like:

> *"By my will the bullies bind,*
> *With focused will and focused mind.*
> *Wherever I go let me see true,*
> *And protective power sticks with me like glue.*
> *I will not be fooled,*
> *I will not be found,*
> *My magic protects me all around!"*

Carry this with you. If you feel you might be in danger, touch the token and repeat the last sentence of the incantation to strengthen the energy, then immediately get help!

Sibling and Parent Serenity

Not everyone has the best relationship with their parents and fewer still even like their siblings. But since all of you have to live under the same roof, you might as well make the best of it. Put on a positive attitude and whip up some peace-keeping magic!

Let's keep this talisman simple. Wait until the Moon is dark (this is a restful time, perfect for leaving behind any bad feelings). Take a white piece of paper (the color of peace) and draw the traditional peace symbol on it. Now, write all the names of everyone who lives in your house (and if you wish those who visit frequently and whose energies may affect your family, positively or negatively). Keep all these names within the boundary of the peace symbol.

Finally, go over the edge of the peace symbol four times with your pen or marker while saying:

> *"Around, within, let peace begin,*
> *Peace affect, peace protect,*
> *Peace begin with me."*

Keep this in a secure place to protect that peace. If possible, locate it near your fireplace or stove (which is the traditional heart of the home). If you can do this, put the symbol inside a fireproof container to be on the safe side.

Study Seeds

Studying isn't that much fun, but if you have to do it anyway, why not combine it with a good snack food and a little magic? The idea behind this charm is to create a bunch of portable munchies that you can nibble on whenever you need a brain boost!

To prepare, you'll need:

- 1 cup of walnuts
- ¼ cup of honey

- An orange-flavored tea bag
- Shredded coconut

Steep the tea bag in two tablespoons of hot water. The idea is to get a concentrated flavor with as little liquid as possible. Next, add the water to your honey and warm, slowly bringing the two to a low rolling boil. Remember to keep your goal in mind all the while you're cooking (focus equals power).

Test the honey to see if it forms soft balls when tiny bits are dropped into a glass of cold water (if your parents ever make candy, have them help). When the honey reaches that stage, toss the nuts into it, and lay them out on waxed paper. Sprinkle with coconut. This is a good time to add your verbal component, something like:

> *"Magic be sure, help me pass this test,*
> *Saturate these nuts with the power of success,*
> *Within each one, my will I bind,*
> *To help me hone my conscious mind."*

These keep for a fairly long time in an airtight container. But if you can't make them yourself, it's perfectly okay to buy some honey-glazed nuts at the store and energize them just the same.

Traffic Talisman

Many of you have learner's permits, are in the process of getting a driver's license, or have your license already. No matter how careful a driver you may be, there's going to be at least a few jerks on the road who are talking on phones, doing their hair, or just not paying attention. Additionally, you're going to meet with all kinds of traffic situations, some of which are just frustrating, and others of which can be dangerous.

Above and beyond being a mindful student driver, it wouldn't hurt to pack some magic in your car. My favorite thing to create is what I call a "portable altar." It's called that because it's a small container that holds one item that represents the four Elements and one item for Spirit. Some suggestions include:

- Small shells or sand for Water (sand can also be Fire)
- A match, ashes, or a red/orange stone for Fire
- A leaf, green stone, soil, or flower petal for Earth
- A feather or incense for Air (incense can also be Fire if burned)
- A white birthday candle for Spirit

Put these in a jar or other container with a good lid and bless them, saying:

*"Air be with me, around me,
and in me for safe movement,
Fire be with me, around me,
and in me for protection,
Water be with me, around me,
and in me for awareness,
Earth be with me, around me,
and in me for wisdom,
Spirit, bless these four, in this container I hold,
To keep me safe on the road."*

If you get in a really sticky situation, you can sprinkle a bit of this mix carefully out your window, but you will have to recreate the amulet later.

Since some of these spells have included specialized timing or birth signs as a key to the process, let's move forward now and take a closer look at astrology and the ways in which it may affect not only your magic but also your life path!

Chapter V

Star Signs:
Applied Astrology

Astrology is a branch of divination that dates back more than four thousand years. From Babylon and Mesopotamia to Greece, Egypt, and India, people (very often the affluent or influential) were literally looking upward for some indication of what the present and future would bring. So much so that the word *horoscope* actually means "observer of time"!

Modern astrology has come a long way from its historical pedestal; now anyone can go online or download an app for their daily horoscopes. While most people no longer use horoscopes to determine when to plant crops, time their travels, or make governmental decisions, there are certainly many who use them for pleasure and daily perspectives. Among this group, we find a growing number of people who look to mystical methods as a way of feeling more in control of the tremendous changes they face daily.

From matters of the heart to group dynamics, this is a very challenging world. Astrology offers a way of tackling these challenges with humor in one hand, spiritual awareness in another, and a little proactive effort tossed in for good measure!

Note that, while Western astrology certainly isn't the only form (for example, the Chinese Zodiac is an alternative), it's the best-known and the one with the most informational resources available. This chapter, therefore, reviews the twelve Western birth signs and provides you with a variety of ideas for applying this information in fun and functional ways.

Aries: March 21–April 19

If you were born during this period, you share your birth sign with Vincent van Gogh, Robert Frost, Mariah Carey, Robert Downey Jr., and Lady Gaga. Being the first sign of the zodiac, Aries tend to want to be at the head of the pack. You are always first in line at the cafeteria or the bus, and the first person to try new things. Better still, Aries make great leaders. When there's a tough project or critical game coming up, you're the person everyone wants and needs on their side because you have an uncanny knack of overcoming the odds. Here's some information about your birth sign:

Lucky Numbers and Days: 1, 9, and Tuesday. Any time you're planning something special, look to Tuesday the 1st, 9th, or 19th (a combination of 1 and 9)!

Aromas That Accent the Positive: Blackberry or marjoram, for relationships. For yourself, go with something as spicy as you are—ginger, clove, neroli, dragon's blood, or frankincense.

School: Aries are usually good students, but only if they're not allowed to get bored. When you're putting together your annual schedules, think variety and challenge, or at least break things up with something that really piques your interest.

Love, Family, and Friendship: Not known for shyness in any way, energy, charm, and charisma make Aries very popular. You don't have to work overly hard to get people to like you—but sometimes your presence can be daunting, as can your sense of competitiveness. Not everyone can keep up with you, so watch that your expectations of others aren't unrealistic. Also take care that you don't act like a Ram, and batter people with ideas or opinions that may not interest them. Overall, your best companions are those born under Leo, Sagittarius, Gemini, and Aquarius.

Power Colors: Reds. You're all fire, and the brighter the better!

Money Matters: Aries typically use money for adventure. They're not overly concerned with riches but with those that help them reach specific goals. (They're nearly as stubborn as Taurus!) You may find this leads to periodic bad moves, but Aries likes risk and can typically get out of trouble when it happens.

Adventure and Entertainment: Aries can become bored quickly, so look to very active sports or other activities requiring ongoing attention and discipline, such as martial arts or step aerobics.

Crystal Clarity: Diamond is your stone, but try a Herkimer (which is far less expensive) to bring out your best. When you need to pace your enthusiasm, go with amethyst for balance. Additionally, red stones such as bloodstone, fire agate, and carnelian bring luck and energy to Aries.

Body Tips: Aries rules the head of the body, meaning pay particular attention to your face and hair. Use shampoos that have some of the aromatics that energize you, like berry scented for happiness, lavender for calm, and orange when you want people to accept you for who you are. Also, consider keeping refreshing face wipes in your locker. The fresher your appearance, the better you feel and think!

Clothes and Jewelry: Always a trendsetter who loves to try new things, use this characteristic in your favor. Find a way to express your vibrant personality within the dress codes of school and work. You can bring flare to anything! Bear in mind that bright colors are best for your energy levels.

The Future: You'll never be a diplomat (bluntness is typical of people born under this sign). However, you can be very successful, happy, and prosperous in nearly any leadership role. Since you can hit the ground running, consider becoming a motivational counselor, a quality-control specialist, or focus on similar careers where you always have a new project on the horizon and where all that drive, aggressiveness, and persistence can really shine.

Taurus: April 20–May 21

If you were born in this period, you share your birth sign with Queen Elizabeth II, William Shakespeare, Cher, and Robert Pattinson. True to the bull-like nature within, the Taurus personality tends to be stubborn and resolute. On one hand, this leads to being resistant to fast changes. On the other, it produces a very reliable, affectionate, and artistic individual. The Taurus is nowhere near as adventurous as an Aries. In fact, you'll probably find yourself drawn to the "status quo" because it's comfortable. There's nothing wrong with this, and for the Bull, it's often best to conform rather than break the proverbial China shop to bits, which is what happens when you feel awkward or uneasy. Here's more information about your sign:

Lucky Numbers and Days: 4, 6, and Friday.

Aromas That Accent the Positive: Woodsy aromas (anything very natural) suit you well. For relationships, consider a blend of pine and clover with a hint of patchouli and vanilla to lift the overall energies surrounding you and your friends. Ylang-ylang is also a good alternative.

School: Stick with the people you know and trust, and don't sweat the rest. Frequently, the Taurus finds that teachers make good friends because they're a "known" element in the whole scheme of things. Also, since you're a creature of habit, give yourself a good morning routine to follow regularly, and most days will go smoothly.

Love, Family, and Friendship: Your best partner is often another Bull who understands your motives and also likes to follow with the herd. Alternatively, Virgo, Capricorn, Pisces, and Cancer all make good companions. Know from the get-go that you won't enjoy overly spontaneous people. Finding security and a sense of place is your game, and anyone who moves too quickly leaves you off balance.

Power Colors: Greens, especially those that have a similar hue to lush vegetation. Also, pale blue or mauve work well.

Money Matters: Hard work is its own reward, and you will be rewarded for yours. Taurus is the great provider of the zodiac. In particular, they do well with real-estate ventures and stretching money to its maximum capacity. If there's a sale to be found or a good bargain, go shopping with a Taurus!

Adventure and Entertainment: In an odd dichotomy, Taurus finds great enjoyment in a thriller book, but not a movie. Epic, emotional flicks are a better choice for a night out on the town with friends. Similarly, rowdy music likely isn't your style. Stick with things that soothe and make you feel comfortable in your space. In terms of sports, you've got lots of stamina, so nearly anything goes.

Crystal Clarity: Your birthstone is emerald, but you can substitute any vibrant green stone. These crystals encourage loyalty in others and protect you from lies. Alternatively, look to pink stones, like kunzite, to keep your spirits upbeat.

Body Tips: Taurus rules the throat, meaning take special care to be sure you don't get colds. Consider gargling every morning with something minty to keep that voice clear. You want (and need) to be heard!

Clothes and Jewelry: Oddly enough, the sometimes-clumsy Bull also has a gentle beauty. You need not fuss that much to be attractive to others. Find clothes that accent your lines, especially your neck. When you really want attention, wear stunning necklaces, especially chokers.

The Future: You will probably enjoy any creative job, especially one in fine arts. Your sense of duty and diligence endears you to employers, so job stability shouldn't prove to be a problem. Additionally, any jobs that deal with money (like banking or finance) are excellent choices for this sign.

Gemini: May 22–June 21

If you were born during this time frame, you share your birth sign with notable people like Marilyn Monroe, Johnny Depp, Natalie Portman, and Chris Evans. The keynotes to the Gemini personality include talkativeness, curiosity, and cleverness, especially with humor. Being an Air sign, Gemini values clarity of thought and action and often brings this clarity into any situation, be it professional or personal. From the outside, this might seem unemotional, but it's not. It's simply your coping mechanism. Here's more information on your sign:

Lucky Numbers and Days: 5, 9, and Wednesday

Aromas That Accent the Positive: For relationships, use mulberry or lily of the valley. For yourself, look to airy aromatics like bergamot, lavender, lemongrass, and mint.

School: Sticking to any one thing is hard for every Gemini, so leave yourself plenty of wiggle room on all your projects. Don't wait until the last minute or you're not likely to finish them. Also, organization isn't your strong suit, so set up your locker with a special area just for clutter. This way, the important stuff is right at hand. Finally, since Gemini likes to constantly be on the go, keep some power bars or other similar snacks handy so you don't burn out.

Love, Family, and Friendship: Gemini tends to be restless, wanting to tackle too many projects at once. This, in turn, can make it hard to maintain relationships. Gemini personalities may also have trouble making decisions and keeping their moods from swinging back and forth erratically. Consequently, it's wise for the Gemini to keep people close who understand this and can help them focus. Also, it's good to consider things like yoga that can help you re-establish balance. The best companions for you are those born under the signs of Leo, Aries, Libra, and Aquarius.

Power Colors: Bright yellow or anything with an opalescent finish so that the surface color keeps changing, meaning it has much-needed novelty appeal.

Money Matters: Budget is a four-letter word to most Geminis. You spend money very easily and really have no idea where it goes. Even so, you're great with finding a bargain and charming people into giving you the best price. The main problem with your spending habits is that you want both practicality and pleasure. In fact, the Twins want it all, so learn how to budget now!

Adventure and Entertainment: Those born under Gemini have a strong love of knowledge and information gathering, and really know how to think on their feet. The Twins also don't like to be bored, and when tedium begins to set in, Geminis will likely set out looking for something to keep their mind busy! I suggest buying collections of short stories or comics, heading to see a comedy movie, hunting down odd trivia, or playing a game of tennis.

Crystal Clarity: Moonstone represents the Gemini personality perfectly in that the Moon waxes and wanes with a similar speed as this personality. If you're looking to accent your luck, carry a pink tourmaline instead.

Body Tips: Gemini rules over the hands. People can't help watching them when you talk, so take good care of them and adorn them well! Also, consider having some good hand lotion in your locker or backpack so your fingers communicate as smoothly as your words!

Clothes and Jewelry: Gemini doesn't make the best fashion statement of the Zodiac by any means. Clothing isn't overly important to you. What is important is comfort. So, stick with denim and other easy-going fabrics that move with you and can handle your pace.

The Future: Geminis have an innate ability to see both sides of any situation or issue and have a natural literary knack. With this in mind, Geminis would do well to consider exploring literary and journalistic endeavors in school and the local community. They can also be effective in any profession that requires strong communication skills, including philosophy, travel, and transportation, or even stand-up comedy! Whatever you choose, however, make sure it offers diversity and ongoing challenges, so the Twins are satisfied and fulfilled.

Cancer: June 22–July 22

If you were born during this time frame, you share your birth sign with notable people like the Dalai Lama, Tom Hanks, Robin Williams, and Selena Gomez. As this list implies, Cancers can be very successful, insightful, creative, and good leaders. Nonetheless, the key quality of the Cancer personality is not being outgoing but delight in the simple pleasures of home and family. Cancers love to retreat into their shells. For this sign, nothing is more highly prized than household harmony. Here's more information on your sign:

Lucky Numbers and Days: 3, 7, and Monday.

Aromas That Accent the Positive: For relationships, agrimony, or jasmine work well. For yourself, look to scents aligned with the Water Element, such as lemon and lily.

School: At school, Cancers often end up with followers as a result of their natural charm. This can be difficult as you'll want private time regularly (and, even then, people "find" you!). Trust those instincts. If you have one social outlet (like the swim team), that will probably be enough.

Love, Family, and Friendship: On the positive side, Cancers make generous, protective friends and family members. You are always there to lend a hand when people need you, and God/dess forbid anyone hurts someone you care about. That's when the Crab comes out with claws open for a fight.

On the downside, because of the strong Water Element here, Cancers have a tendency to be overly sensitive, emotional, very stubborn, sulking, and vindictive (none of which usually provide the results you want). You laugh easily, cry easily, get hurt easily, and, when faced with not getting your own way, you'll want to retreat into your shell until you're ready to play or work again. This shell often equates to a secret place—a spot near the water where you can heal and refresh. If you don't have one already, find one. Your best companions are those born under the signs of Scorpio, Pisces, Capricorn, and Virgo.

Power Colors: Silver, pale blue, and sea green (or anything else that reminds you of the Moon or water).

Money Matters: Cancers are very adept in both making and managing money because they treasure security. With this in mind, combined with your homebody nature, you would do well to look into various "backyard" tasks through which you can earn some fun money. Depending on your living environment, there are plenty of possibilities. Sit down with your family and discuss what they want and need, then bargain out a price in a typical Cancer manner! Also, open a bank account so you can put that money to work for you.

Adventure and Entertainment: Romantic books, happily-ever-after movies, retro music, and eating out are all high on Cancer's list of enjoyable activities. In terms of sports, look to swimming or other aquatics.

Crystal Clarity: Your birthstone is ruby, but as with other signs, you can utilize nearly any red or pink stone to accent the best of the Cancer attributes. In particular, an agate with this hue draws good fortune. Also, moonstone is a good choice because of its association with water. (When you can't get close to a pond or ocean, use the crystal as a calming influence.)

Body Tips: Cancer rules the stomach (and sometimes your stomach rules you). It's not uncommon for Cancers to have a passion for good food, even if it's food that's not really "good" for you. So, be mindful of your choices, and consider a good holistic exercise program that fits into your schedule.

Clothes and Jewelry: Trends don't faze the Crab in the least. You want to wear what you like and what feels good. You have clothes that are tattered and torn, but you can't bear to part with them and would rather shop secondhand than spend a fortune on something new. Be aware, however, that comfort doesn't mean you have to give up looking good. Dress up your wardrobe with wraps or jewelry, especially anything with pearls in it.

The Future: In looking to the future, the Cancer love for food might lead to a career as a chef. Alternatively, Cancers tend to feel strongly about their country and often go into public service (like the military or politics). A good third option for any Cancer is a career that either involves working with money (accounting, banking) or keeps them near the water, like marine biology or professional water sports.

Leo: July 23–August 21

If you were born during this period, you share your birth sign with notable people like Neil Armstrong, Madonna, Dua Lipa, and Shawn Mendes. Leos love the spotlight and have the necessary personal charisma to take on public roles with seeming ease. Just like kings and queens of the concrete jungle, they are very determined, which allows them to accomplish almost anything to which they set their minds. In fact, the bigger the project, the better, for these fiercely status-oriented lions. Here's more about your sign:

Lucky Numbers and Days: 8, 9, and Sunday.

Aromas That Accent the Positive: For relationships, use sage or marigold. For personal aromatics, consider scents that are fiery like you—orange, frankincense, cinnamon, and ginger are four examples.

School: Constantly seeking attention as you sometimes do can be bothersome to others. Your natural charm and charisma will work for you without your pushing yourself on people. In fact, being a little aloof presents an air of mystery that makes people curious. Know your jungle, pace it out, but remember that you're not really the ruler here—just a very intense guest.

Love, Family, and Friendship: Despite their driven personality, Leos are warm and approachable, making them well-loved by many. The only real problem comes when their integrity is questioned—and then watch out. The inner Lion will roar and bite the person perceived as being the source of the accusation whether or not they're the actual source of the statement or rumor. When this happens, Leo should stop and take a breath and make sure their anger is being directed accurately or they may end up damaging a friendship forever. Good companions for Leos include Libras, Geminis, and Aries.

Power Colors: Since Leo is ruled by the sun, look to gold, bronze, and orange hues to really energize that lion-heart.

Money Matters: In particular, Leo excels in financial ventures, having amazing luck with money (and loving the glow of coins). They are also resourceful, knowing how to balance out even an excess of spending or losses. With this in mind, those born under this sign would do well to develop investing and entrepreneurial abilities during their teen years. The only caution is being aware that a Leo's idealism, generosity, and pride can sometimes undermine their goals. Idealism puts on "rose-colored glasses" toward situations that could use scrutiny. Generosity may lead to having hard-earned money go out without the expectation of a solid return. Finally, pride works hand-in-hand with a Leo's ideals, as they want to be in control, decisive, and expect others to follow. This means any financial decisions require slow, patient consideration rather than a lion's pounce.

Adventure and Entertainment: Dramatic or romantic —and very little in between—pleases the Leo's need for entertainment. In terms of adventure, if you're going to travel it's in style (nothing goes unattended). Musically, you like artists who show longevity (none of those industry plants for you)! And, in sports, nearly anything goes. You love a good, fair competition.

Crystal Clarity: Tiger's eye (of course) and sunstone all please the Lion, who loves a little flash. But these crystals also empower the solar aspect of your sign, giving you greater presence and control.

Body Tips: Leos are very body-conscious, so it wouldn't surprise me if you already have a workout program. Just be aware that not everyone is as physically competitive as you, and don't think less of them because of that. Also, Leo rules over the back, so make sure you pay particular attention to strengthening that region in your exercises and remember to visualize a sparkling white light pouring into your mane from above. This improves confidence and also brings protective energy to bear.

Clothes and Jewelry: It's a natural tendency for Leos to preen. They flourish in bright, bold colors, sassy clothes, and anything else that draws attention. The more expensive, the better, but on your budget that's not always possible. So, find other ways to jazz up your clothes with small, vibrant accents.

The Future: In looking to the future, Leos do well in any leadership role, especially one tied to an idealistic vision.

Using investments to establish and run a charity would be one good example. Leos also do well in jobs where they work with what most of us consider luxury items, like owning their own antique or designer clothing shop. Finally, because of the Lion's love of the spotlight, any entertainment field is also a great place for Leos to shine.

Virgo: August 22–September 23

You share your birth sign with notable people like Sean Connery, Mother Teresa, Stephen King, Keanu Reeves, and Beyoncé. The keynotes to the Virgo personality include creativity, helpfulness, loyalty, meticulousness, and a strong sense of responsibility. Here is more information about your sign:

Lucky Numbers and Days: 3, 5, and Wednesday.

Aromas That Accent the Positive: For relationships, use cedar or lavender. Honeysuckle, cypress, and lemon balm are good personal choices when you want your service and objective-oriented demeanor to shine.

School: Where your Gemini friends are busily gathering information, you're the one who finds a way to analyze and use it. You can take what you're given, toss out what you don't need, and then immediately apply the rest. Those born under this sign strive for perfection, retain knowledge very well, and are very politically and socially mindful in their interactions. This makes a Virgo ideal for student council positions because they want to feel useful, will be honest about their goals, and follow through on promises!

Love, Family, and Friendship: If you want follow-through on any project, Virgo is the sign to look to for help. Virgos are very intent on practicality and hard work, giving attention to planning and details, thinking through decisions, and remaining honest in all their dealings. The only caution in this birth sign is being aware that not everyone can live up to their expectations and concept of perfection. A note to all Virgos: Don't get overly critical, and don't pour yourself so much into your work that you forget to relax and have fun! Without that balance, Virgos can become cranky, worrisome workaholics, or terribly pessimistic. Good companions for them include Capricorns, Scorpios, and Pisces.

Power Colors: Navy blues and gray (and anything that represents personal refinement and good taste).

Money Matters: Virgos hate to borrow or lend money. Their checkbooks are always balanced and they're very frugal, feeling the best things in life truly are free (and they always find the freebies!). They are always self-reliant in this area, preferring to accumulate less tangible things like good friends.

Adventure and Entertainment: Books of facts (especially hard-to-find information) are a great joy for this sign. Similarly, with movies, Virgos would rather not waste time with things that don't somehow improve one's life. Musically, you like to know what a song says and means, while in sports, you'll seek after something that combines both mental and physical stimulation, like gymnastics and hang gliding. On the other hand, you're kind of high-strung, and you don't want to feed that tension. Be aware of how your "play" time influences your thoughts and feelings. As far as travel goes, you always have a good time, but only if everyone follows your schedule. You'll never be late, but also grow impatient with those who lag behind.

Crystal Clarity: Your lucky stones are carnelian and sardonyx. If you're looking for some peace of mind, however, wear something with a sapphire in it.

Body Tips: Virgo rules the nervous system, so you may want to avoid anything with too much caffeine. You have enough drive for two people, and the caffeine only increases that drive (Unless, of course, you want to paint a whole house in one day!).

Clothes and Jewelry: Virgos pay close attention to what they wear and how they wear it. Typically, you prefer a few high-quality items over dozens of cheap things that go the way of fads. In particular, you like sporty clothing and would do well to wear more of it since it energizes you. To save time (since you know you'll do it anyway), iron your clothes before bed and put them where you can dress quickly and efficiently. Stick with natural colors and fabrics, as those are the most comfortable. You don't need a lot of jewelry to make you happy—one piece, well worn, is quite fine.

The Future: The Virgo eye for detail and strong work ethic work in your favor in nearly any environment, but where you feel something is inequitable or unfair you're likely to move on. In particular, Virgos succeed in jobs where they can analyze the situation and then proactively apply lifelong skills—for example, as a computer analyst, technical editor, dietician, or personal assistant.

Libra: September 24–October 22

If you were born during this period, you share your sign with such notables as Mahatma Gandhi, Aleister Crowley, Oscar Wilde, Serena Williams, and Jenna Ortega.

Libra represents the eternal partner of the Zodiac, never really liking aloneness. Libras seek strong, long-term relationships that provide harmony and joy to both people. Additionally, as can be deduced from the symbol of the scales, Libras constantly struggle for balance and order. When these cannot be established, the typically easygoing demeanor of the Libra goes by the wayside until the situation is resolved. Here's more information about your sign:

Lucky Numbers and Days: 6, 9, and Friday.

Aromas That Accent the Positive: For relationships, bergamot or geranium are ideal. Additional scents that accentuate your positive attributes include vanilla, daffodil, geranium, and pine.

School: A Libra personality may find themselves pulled in two directions at the same time and always by equally appealing choices. This inner battle gets tiresome, especially in school, where people are constantly presenting them with options. To help make decisions without waffling, get a coin minted in the year you were born and keep it in your locker or backpack. When you feel vacillation setting in, flip the coin. If the head side comes up, it means your initial gut instinct was a good one, so follow it. If the tails side comes up, stop where you are. This is the "just don't go there" signal.

Love, Family, and Friendship: Librans are fantastic diplomats; they constantly seek harmony and understanding. This either endears them to people or infuriates folks because while Librans are sociable, cheerful, and charming people, indecision is a huge problem for them. They dislike taking sides. This again is where having a divination tool like the coin or other binary system (yes/no, stay/go) comes in handy. While I wouldn't suggest relying on it too often (you need logic and intuition in any choices presented), it will help when you're really stuck. Better still, once you've made a choice it makes everyone else feel better—as yours is typically a deciding vote! Good companions for you are those born under the signs of Aquarius, Leo, Gemini, and Sagittarius.

Power Colors: Royal blue and rose pink (and when one is balanced against the other, the results double).

Money Matters: Libras love comfort and luxury, and consequently they're often short on money, having spent it on their latest acquisition. Don't take out car or student loans unless you have someone better with the budget than yourself to help keep the bills paid on time.

Adventure and Entertainment: Most Libras enjoy physical activity but are often carried away by fads, so think before you leap into that next yoga class or set of roller skates. Really, what you want more than the activity is socialization! Anything you enjoy doing is much better when you have a companion. For reading, mushy romance novels seem to be the genre of choice, whereas movies run the full spectrum so long as you have someone with whom to watch them.

Crystal Clarity: Your lucky stones are opal and chrysolite. You might also want to carry one black and one white stone in your power pouch to accent the Libra sense of symmetry.

Body Tips: Libra rules over the backside and kidney area. Since you like physical activity anyway, find an exercise that works that area.

Clothes and Jewelry: Libras have a great deal of self-confidence, and that shows in the way you present yourself. Quite honestly, you can turn heads wearing a potato sack, let alone something you really like. So, rather than fussing every day, just pick out your clothes a week in advance and line them up in the closet. It will alleviate a lot of decision-making. During your fun free time, wear clothes that show off your midriff—it's bound to catch some admiring glances!

The Future: Libras can struggle with work because they prefer ideal environments in which to apply themselves. Nonetheless, as a seeker of truth and justice who enjoys a good exchange of ideas, advisory positions, or those requiring negotiating skills, are well suited to Libra sensibilities. Look to a career path in law, counseling, or something similar.

Scorpio: October 23–November 21

You share your birth sign with notable people like Marie Antoinette, Marie Curie, Sylvia Plath, Kiernan Shipka, and Ciara. The keynotes to the Scorpio personality include determination, adventure, charisma, compulsiveness, and secretiveness. Scorpios are also very strong-minded, sensitive, passionate, and goal-oriented. Here's more information about your sign:

Lucky Numbers and Days: 2, 4, and Tuesday.

Aromas That Accent the Positive: For relationships, use basil or patchouli. Otherwise, try geranium, hyacinth, and fresh-picked woodruff.

School: You're mystical and magnetic, hardworking, and sometimes very demanding (especially with yourself). While you're still in high school, see if you can't apply that energy to some volunteer work in keeping with your personal career goals for the future! These types of efforts make for great resume builders, provide job skills, and help when you're competing for the National Honor Society, scholarships, or college placements. Additionally, you may find that some types of service like Greenpeace or the Peace Corps could allow you to reach out far beyond your backyard to other parts of the world!

Love, Family, and Friendship: Once you set your sights on something specific, it's likely you'll follow through 150 percent! So, why not use that upbeat, positive energy to do something good for someone else? You can get involved in special school functions or community service, and these are ideal places to let your talents shine. There are also a lot of adults who could benefit from your natural empathy—namely the elderly. Scorpios tend to be "old souls" in that you usually relate to adults better than people your own age anyway. Your honesty, warmth, and realness appeal to the elderly and can give them a lot of happy moments that might have otherwise been spent alone. Your best companions are those born under Cancer, Virgo, Capricorn, or Pisces.

Power Colors: Absolute black or vibrant red, and in combination—can you say *wow!* Also, crimson, burgundy, and maroon (to show off your passionate side).

Money Matters: For you, money is a means of obtaining control, security, and most of all a sense of freedom. You're more than happy to work hard and give up a few things if it gets you closer to those goals.

Adventure and Entertainment: Scorpios don't relish sports or athletics unless they're highly competitive and challenging. When traveling, think exotic and enthralling (like a mystery-thriller train ride), and for reading pleasure while you're waiting for action, get horror or dark fantasy.

Crystal Clarity: Your lucky stones are aquamarine and beryl.

Body Tips: Scorpio rules over the genitals, meaning you really have to be careful to discriminate between real feelings versus hormone-inspired charges (especially until your brain finishes developing). Take a deep breath and think seriously before diving into anything you might not really be ready for.

Clothes and Jewelry: Wear things that make you seem even more mysterious than the Scorpio personality projects already. Don't let anyone predict you or pin down your style. Outfits from other eras, sunglasses, and unique shirts that make people wonder "what's that about?" are all perfect for your personality.

The Future: In looking to the future, the community service you put in during high school will prove very helpful to a Scorpio. In thinking about college, look for classes that can help you in management and/or problem-solving jobs, including counseling. Alternatively, consider a career where you're working to improve the environment, specifically clean-up and preservation. A third option is any specialized health field, including nutrition, sports injuries, and massage therapy.

Sagittarius: November 22–December 21

You share your birth sign with notable people like Walt Disney, Emily Dickinson, Taylor Swift, and Billie Eilish. The keynotes to the Sagittarius personality include an optimistic outlook, honesty, willpower, tolerance, and a great love of nature. The Sagittarius personality often boasts a contagious sense of humor, empathy, and charm, but also requires a lot of activity to keep that upbeat demeanor going. Here's more information about your sign:

Lucky Numbers and Days: 5, 7, and Thursday.

Aromas That Accent the Positive: For relationships, use dandelion or hyssop. For personal aromatics, look no further than the pantry for nutmeg, clove, saffron, and rosemary.

School: You might think about becoming an exchange student. This is a great way to experience other cultures firsthand, with all the flavor and intensity Sagittarians love. Ask your guidance counselor about the options offered by your school along these lines.

Love, Family, and Friendship: Sagittarians need a lot of change to keep them happy. Adventure, moving, and travel all hold great appeal. You may want to seriously look into taking trips with family and friends over winter, spring, and summer breaks or finding other ways to see the world. The only caution in traveling with others is that your Sagittarius personality is prone to possessiveness, and you are sometimes overly blunt to the point of hurting others, even when that's not what you meant to do. So, in any ongoing interactions, periodically take some downtime alone to decompress. Your best companions are Leo, Libra, Aries, and Aquarius.

Power Colors: Midnight blue or royal purple (anything regal).

Money Matters: Whether things are good or not so good, you tend to see the bright side. Many people born under this sign have uncanny luck with finances. While you may never really worry about money, you have this sense that everything will work out (as it usually does) and would much rather focus on other matters.

Adventure and Entertainment: Sagittarians love upbeat and rhythmic sounds. For some outdoor activities, how about an old-fashioned hike in a nearby forest? This is an all-weather adventure that generally requires nothing more than a backpack, proper clothing, and good shoes! It also appeals to your love of the outdoors. When time allows for any type of travel, definitely go for the slower transportation options, like boat and train. Sagittarians generally want to experience everything fully—it's all about the journey, not necessarily the destination.

Crystal Clarity: Turquoise is a great choice, as it provides you with an improved perspective. Lucky stones are topaz and pearl.

Body Tips: This sign rules over the hips and thighs, so find a way to accent those parts of yourself. Wear low-rise jeans and a flashy belt. This is also your center of gravity, and wearing something weighty in that region helps the Sagittarian to feel focused even when on the move.

Clothes and Jewelry: Since Sagittarians love athletics and tend toward a high-paced lifestyle, dress with your activities in mind. Wear shoes that allow you to hit the floor running (literally) and various types of sportswear that you find comfortable. By the way, comfort doesn't mean boring—bright colors suit your outlook and keep you vibrant.

The Future: In looking to the future, any traveling you did during your teen years will provide you with good global insights into people and situations. You can apply this wisdom and your personable nature to positions like counseling others, selling any services or products in which you believe, researching nearly any topic (hey, knowledge is power), or maybe even becoming a travel agent so other people can enjoy all the adventures you have! If you can find a career along these lines where travel is required, all the better. You will always be happier on the road and moving toward new horizons.

Capricorn: December 22–January 20

You share your birth sign with such notable people as Alexander Hamilton, David Bowie, Greta Thunberg, and Timothée Chalamet. The keynotes to the Capricorn personality include great patience, a very even disposition, strong convictions, good negotiating and organizational skills, practical precaution in any undertaking, methodical approaches to problems, a well-developed sense of responsibility, and a strong work ethic. Here's more information about your sign:

Lucky Numbers and Days: 2, 8, and Saturday.

Aromas That Accent the Positive: For relationships, try comfrey or bay. For yourself, go with something as adaptable and sure-footed as are you—vetiver. Alternatively, you may find any musky aroma has a similar effect.

School: Capricorns are the most stable, serious, independent, and confident of all the zodiac signs. All these attributes combine in Capricorns to create an ideal leader who can concentrate on tasks and get the job done. Consider getting involved in a school project or activity where you can take charge and make things happen!

Love, Family, and Friendship: Don't become too serious, rigid, or traditional in your ways—especially with people close to you. Remain flexible and don't expect that everyone around you can maintain your pace and focus. When you find you're having trouble with loosening up, switch from your typical earth-toned clothing to something brighter, and that should help. Also remember to use your sense of humor as an ally. You have a way of turning phrases that can bring smiles and relieve a lot of tension. Your best companions are those born under Taurus, Virgo, Scorpio, or Pisces.

Power Colors: Look to earth tones, particularly dark green and brown.

Money Matters: Capricorns are shrewd with money. You look at any job or situation as an opportunity, and take the slow, steady route to success. There is no chance of being fooled by get-rich-quick scams, as you're somewhat pessimistic anyway! If you set your mind to making money, you will.

Adventure and Entertainment: Looking at your personal shelves, you're likely to find factual accounts, drama, and work-oriented books or movies. For sports, either look to something that's a real challenge to a goat (rock climbing) or to a team sport like soccer to provide the competition on which you thrive.

Crystal Clarity: Lapis, fluorite, and amethyst all accent the diligent Capricorn personality and provide a sense of feeling good in your skin.

Body Tips: Capricorn rules knees, bones, and joints, which is interesting because your steady, consistent nature protects those very parts. You're not likely to jump into any high-impact exercises but go with sound long-term routines to keep yourself looking and feeling your best.

Clothes and Jewelry: Go with classic cuts, power pieces, and understated jewelry. This approach says "success" without boasting. Your personality carries everything else.

The Future: In looking to the future, the leadership positions you obtain in high school will prove very helpful to Capricorn's career path. In thinking about college, look for classes that can continue to improve your management and/or problem-solving skills, and take at least one class that is just for fun! Careers in network administration for a cutting-edge software firm, managing a budget-wise restaurant, or being an engineer for earthquake-zone buildings are all good examples of jobs in which Capricorns can excel.

Aquarius: January 21–February 19

You share your birth sign with such notable people as Mozart, Charles Darwin, Shakira, and Harry Styles. The keynotes to the Aquarian personality include idealism, a love of social interaction, adventure, unpredictability, and strong communication skills. Aquarians are also very intellectual, humanitarian, and the type of folks who like to live life to its fullest, not simply sit on the sidelines. Here's more information about your sign:

Lucky Numbers and Days: 1, 7, and Wednesday.

Aromas That Accent the Positive: For relationships, anise or wisteria work well. To augment your Aquarian attributes, use lavender, violet, lemon verbena, or galbanum.

School: People born under this sign often express their zeal through the arts—the performing arts, in particular—because they offer an ongoing challenge to the mind and soul. While rarely leaders (Aquarians hate being the "boss"), their natural aptitude inspires everyone with whom they come in contact. With this in mind, it's well worth exploring the arts that are represented at your school, including things like drama club.

The arts that Aquarians love take time and tenacity to achieve excellence, but they should take care to avoid getting so caught up in their artistic endeavors that they overlook homework, after-school jobs, or family responsibilities. Excellence in the arts often means working with "experts" that most Aquarians find annoying, no matter how helpful they try to be. Remember here that you can learn a lot from experts and still develop your own style. Listen to your mentors while working on quelling your rebellious aspects (or at least keeping them in check), and you could find real genius.

Love, Family, and Friendship: Aquarians have trouble moderating personal inventive flow versus their overactive sense of devotion—in other words, they're either "on" or "off" with surrounding people and projects, and there's little middle ground. Consequently, it's a good idea to periodically take a break from people and give themselves a breather. While you might like working with others because it gives you the chance to make friends (something not all Aquarians find easy to do), you have an independent and empathic spirit that you need to nurture, too. Your best companions are those born under Gemini, Libra, Aries, and Sagittarius.

Power Colors: Electric or sky blue. Also, anything with rainbow hues.

Money Matters: Money is not the driving force in your life. Oh, sure, it's useful for important personal projects, but typically you'd rather barter than buy. You hate borrowing, and if you lend, you expect to be paid on time. One rather interesting gift, however, is that you do have some luck with money and small amounts will show up quite unexpectedly.

Adventure and Entertainment: Sci-fi or futuristic movies and books will keep you captivated for whole days when time allows. Musically, seek out global sounds that reflect your global-minded nature (world rhythms come immediately to mind). Any sport in which you participate must be cutting-edge, be it snowboarding or bungee jumping!

Crystal Clarity: Your lucky stones are amethyst and garnet, especially if set in silver.

Body Tips: Aquarius rules over the ankles and the circulatory system. So, make sure you have good, supportive shoes and boots, and consider aerobics to keep your circulation at its best. A bloodstone makes an excellent portable charm that supports this goal (and, in fact, it was once used as a magical treatment for blood problems).

Clothes and Jewelry: Most Aquarians feel happy in loose, flowy clothes—anything interesting, unique, and comfortable. Also, decorate those ankles—put bells on and ring out your arrival everywhere you go!

The Future: In looking to the future (something Aquarians love to plan for), stick with careers you feel strongly about (Aquarians tend to have very powerful convictions). Avoid positions that might require dishonesty like sales, as these just don't suit you and will quickly make you unhappy to the point of distraction. On the other hand, anything that benefits humankind and allows you to apply your intellect and creativity, like the sciences, natural history, or photography, will prove very successful.

Pisces: February 20th–March 20

Dear Pisces, you have a very big heart that often overwhelms your head. This makes almost all your relationships really intense—sometimes good and sometimes bad. There is very little middle ground for people close to you: you're either dissing them or applauding. The good news is that the people you love know without a doubt that you do so completely. This is also true of anything that you care about, be it sports, art, or a political ideal. When you care about something, you wrap yourself in it, and rarely let go. You share your birth sign with Albert Einstein, Steve Irwin, Justin Bieber, and Millie Bobby Brown. Here is more information about your sign:

Lucky Numbers and Days: 2, 6, and Friday.
Aromas That Accent the Positive: For relationships, try hyacinth and jasmine. For yourself, look to lily, ylang-

ylang, apple, and ambergris, or anything that reminds you of the sea.

School: Pisces are very creative, which will make or break your educational focus. Some apply this creativity for success, while others find it downright distracting. If you are in the second category, you can turn things around without losing that spark. For one, try surrounding yourself with the aroma of rosemary and toning down the wardrobe a bit so you look and feel more serious. For another, experiment with a variety of educational paths until you find the "right" one. Typically, the first career Pisces thinks they want disappears in college and a better life path appears.

Love, Family, and Friendship: Unfortunately, the Piscean tendency toward extreme love and passion can mean stubbornly holding on to those things that may not be good for you. It often happens when someone points this out to you, proud Pisces says, "I don't think so!" Keep this in mind, especially when family and friends are trying to help. It doesn't mean you have to take their advice all the time, but at least try to listen with a more open mind. Remember: You're a Pisces, not a Taurus. You don't need to be bullheaded. Release, listen, consider, then decide.

Along the same lines, your natural creativity often means you're a daydreamer, which can get you in trouble. People tell you to get your head out of the clouds when they don't understand the amazing things you see there. Nonetheless, tighten up your mind and know that you really have the power to make life what you want it. Once you find the right outlet for all that creativity, you'll be incredibly successful, and some of those daydreams will come true. Your best companions are those born under Cancer, Scorpio, Taurus, or Capricorn.

Power Colors: All shades of blue and purple please the watery Pisces, but most find purple the predominant hue for energy. Another good color is sea green.

Money Matters: Saving for a rainy day is not in the Pisces' nature. Even those who are strongly security-oriented find that desired security in their willpower, not in cash on hand. The quest or dream is more important to you than the reward, as is freedom. If there's a way to make money while pursuing those two goals—perfect!

Adventure and Entertainment: Romantic, dramatic, and imaginative books and movies capture Pisces' attention very quickly. Your musical tastes tend to be eclectic—everything from movie themes to sea shanties! For sports, trust in your fishy nature and go swimming, water skiing, or surfing.

Crystal Clarity: Lucky stones include amethyst, blue lace agate, and fluorite. Also, anything that comes from the sea (shells and pearls) accents your dreamy, imaginative nature.

Body Tips: As a Pisces, your power is in your eyes and feet. You can charm, taunt, teach, and tell whole stories with nothing more than a glance. You can also readily walk away from those things that seem uninteresting, unhealthy, or just plain dumb. To accent your eyes, choose a variety of colored sunglasses. Dark ones mean business. To anyone looking at a Pisces wearing these (especially on a cloudy day), they say: "Stay away; I'm not in the mood!" Bright colors imply that you're happy and ready to have some fun. Rose-colored glasses are great for when you only want to see the best in everything around you or to lift a gloomy mood.

It's very important for you to wear good shoes. As a Pisces, you're bound to have regular bouts of insecurity or uncertainty. Strong, sturdy shoes will give you a greater sense of physical balance, which also translates into metaphysical reality. These shoes don't have to be boring. Dress them up and let them communicate what you may not be saying with your words! A well-supported set of heels says, "Look and appreciate, but don't touch without permission! If you do, the heel will end up in your face!" Sneakers imply that you're ready to run or walk on the wild side and are just waiting for a good opportunity.

Clothes and Jewelry: Pisces are very free spirits who like to have clothing that's as free and unconstrained as their imagination. While some people might look at you and wonder about the fashion statement you're making, you know exactly what you want to say and how you want to communicate it through your wardrobe. Nonetheless, everyone has days when they're not feeling fully "on." This is the time to get a little outrageous and daring. Mix colors and textures. Be playful! And look to lightweight fabrics that will keep you feeling unconfined and independent.

On Monday, go with silver or white highlights to honor the Moon, which is important to Pisceans. On Tuesday, you can turn to yellow hues to improve your ability to connect with more logical matters, like studying. Wednesday is a fire day—wear orange or bright yellow and put all that energy into your favorite pastime. Thursday turns your attention to those things you hate doing but have to do anyway. Wear a color that keeps you on task. Friday is the heart day for Pisceans, and you will inevitably feel more of everything on this day of the week. If you feel sad when you wake up, go for something bright to lighten the mood. If you're overly happy to the point of distraction, tone it down with dark accents. And, since Saturday and Sunday are the weekend—hey, wing it! Pisceans love spontaneity.

The Future: Pisces are the explorers of the zodiac, both complex and idealistic. Truth, beauty, justice, and fair play must be part of this picture professionally. The Piscean will love anything with a spiritual or mystical bend and find this focus financially fulfilling too. Alternatively, anything charity-oriented, or positions that allow the expression of inner vision, such as design or acting, are good choices for a career path.

This has been a very short review of a very complex art. If you'd like to learn more and explore your birth sign and those of friends or family more closely, I'd suggest Linda Goodman's *Sun Signs* (written for an adult crowd, but very informative and with a good sense of humor), or *Teen Astrology* by M. J. Abadie. Together, these two books make a really good foundation for learning about astrology in ways that you can immediately apply to your daily life.

Chapter VI

Future-Telling: Divination Made Easy

Divination was developed by our ancestors because they (like us) wanted to feel more in control of their fate, not to mention that they were curious about the future. At first, divination was all about watching the world and trying to connect things that were happening to potential future occurrences. Since our ancestors saw nature as the fingerprint of the gods and a reflection of universal truths, that's where most people's attention turned. They listened to the wind, observed cloud formations, and watched the movement of various animals. Every storm, every falling star, and literally hundreds of other occurrences were cataloged and assigned a meaning based on repeated experience.

At first, this approach may sound a little silly, but in truth, science still depends heavily on observation as a key to unlocking various mysteries. To give you an example of where divination and science meet on common ground, let's look at the belief that a swallow flying low means that it's going to rain. This is a simple bird omen, but one proven to be true. Apparently, when it rains, the insects the swallow prey upon move lower into the atmosphere—and the birds are just following their lunch! So, science has allowed us to see that some of these divination methods are backed up by sound reasoning and, therefore, were often correct.

The purpose of this chapter is to provide you with some sound divination methods that you can readily use nearly anywhere, at any time. Like our ancestors, we're going to depend on creativity, observation, and tried-and-true methods to help yield successful results. Copy the ones you like the most (and find to be most accurate for you) into your Book of Shadows.

Me, a Diviner?

I suspect at least a few of you readers are wondering how you can become your own diviner, especially if you've never considered yourself particularly psychic. First, relax. Nothing I share here is overly difficult. It may take some time and practice to find which method works best for you and to start getting accurate readings regularly, but everyone can do this!

No matter the tools involved, divination is all about tapping into your inner awareness and, through that, gaining more universal perspectives. Think of this like tuning into a frequency on a radio. You're shifting your personal energies and tuning into the frequency you need to answer a question or get a peek into the future.

How each person best accomplishes this differs, but here is a basic pattern that seems to work for many:

1. Once you find a system (the tarot, runes, or whatever) that appeals to you, bless and charge any needed item regularly (information on blessing and charging is in Chapter Four). Carry it with you so it begins to respond to your energy signa-

ture (this is one of the reasons people sometimes ask that you not touch their tarot deck).
2. Try to memorize the symbols in your system. While you can certainly read the meanings in a book, I find that constantly having to refer back to a book can be distracting and cumbersome. Additionally, the memorization process allows you to personalize the system as you go—if there's a card or stone that means something different to you from the meaning given by the creator of that system indicates, always defer to your personal interpretation.
3. Prepare yourself. Take time to breathe, pray, or meditate. Perhaps wash your hands to get rid of any residual energy collected there (random energies can cling to our hands throughout the day). This is a good time to check your intentions and overall state of mind and body. Just like with spells, divination won't be very positive or successful if you're angry, ill, or out of sorts.
4. Add candles or aromatics to the process for ambiance. This is really to help set the mood, which can make a huge difference to your mindset.
5. Turn off the phone or find a private spot to work to avoid disruption and distraction.
6. Think about your question in as much detail as possible. Use focus and willpower.
7. Follow the instructions for casting or laying out your given system.
8. Read the results you get—you'll want to write these down so you can gauge accuracy.
9. It may take up to six months or more of working with any system to get really good at it. In particular, the tarot is tricky because it contains

so many symbols. Just be patient with yourself. You're nurturing both your inner psychic and witch in this process, and it will take as long as it takes!

Choosing a System

Discussing the numerous symbols in the tarot brings up a very common question—namely, how do you go about finding the "right" system? Considering there are hundreds of tarot decks, various oracles, runes, stones, and probably about three hundred systems (of which I'm aware) using everything from sticks to clouds, it's not like you can try everything! Here are a few possible methods.

Traditional Divination Systems

Just for fun, here's a list of some of the things our ancestors observed or used to get insights into their present and future circumstances:

- **Aeromancy:** clouds and atmospheric phenomena, observed
- **Alectormancy:** roosters picking at grain, observed
- **Bibliomancy:** books, randomly chosen phrases
- **Botanomancy:** branches, burning
- **Capnomancy:** smoke from a sacred fire, patterns observed
- **Chalcomancy:** brass or copper bowls, striking and listening
- **Cromniomancy:** onions, grown and observed
- **Dactylomancy:** fingers or rings, observed
- **Daphnomancy:** laurel leaves, the sounds made when burned
- **Felidomancy:** cats, observed

- **Gelomancy:** laughter, interpreted sounds
- **Halomancy:** salt, cast on a fire
- **Myomancy:** mice, actions of those suddenly appearing
- **Omphalomancy:** belly button, contemplating
- **Ovomancy:** eggs on water, shapes formed by
- **Rhabdomancy:** rods, water witching
- **Sciomancy:** moon, appearance or phase
- **Sciomancy:** shadow, size and shape of
- **Transataumancy:** overheard phrases or events witnessed accidentally

And that's just the tip of the iceberg. Other forms of divination call for arrows, bones, crystals, dice, coins, ink, wax, tea leaves, palms, feathers, and numbers!

First, ask yourself what sense you respond to most strongly. Visual people will like tarot or similar pictorial systems because they're visually inspiring, or they may like to turn to old-fashioned methods, like observing animal behavior. People who respond to touch might like runes or stones better. People with keen hearing might look to various listening systems (the wind, the leaves, water, or even earth movements).

Second, let your inner voice guide you. As you're looking through various options at the store, stop and extend your psychic, witchy self. Do you like what you see and what you're reading? It helps if you can see an open set and fully experience how the system may work, but not every store offers that option. You can also check customer reviews on Amazon or other websites.

Also, do you have a friend who might be able to let you try their similar system before you buy? This could save you a ton of time, money, and aggravation. I once thought I really liked a deck but couldn't find an open one. When I saw all the cards, I was very disappointed.

It just didn't "feel" right—the symbols were flat to me (low impact). I ended up giving this set away to someone who loved it (which is fine to do, by the way). But that was an expensive mistake (tarot decks can be costly), and one you don't need to make.

Another way to find out more about divination systems and see them up close is to go to a psychic fair. Here you can observe numerous readers and tools to get a better idea of what you might want to use and how to use it. These fairs are a great indicator of just how individualized our community has become in its magical approaches. Each reader has their own way of working with the tools they have, and each may read the same system completely differently!

In any case, definitely shop around, take your time, and wait until something speaks to you deeply. If you find you're uncertain about the system after you've purchased it, give it a few months of trial time. Some systems take time to warm up to—within about three months, you should notice your feelings about it should have improved, as will your results. If not, I'd say you didn't get the right thing. Just do what I did: pass along that divination tool to someone who loves it and keep hunting.

I finally settled on the *Whimsical Tarot* by Dorothy Morrison, a set of runes, and a personally devised system called the Sacred Stone Oracle.

Making Your Own Divination System

Since I just spoke about personally devised systems, you might like to know a little bit more about how to make a divination tool. This is especially true if you're not having any luck finding one that really speaks to your higher self.

The first question to ask yourself is if you want to base your tools on an existing system that you adapt or create something new. I think most people like to use a pre-existing construct just because it's a little easier than starting from scratch. If you're going to use a system like runes or tarot as your starting point, get some information on how many symbols you'll need, as this becomes important in step two—finding your media. With tarot, for example, you need seventy-two symbols, whereas with runes, you can work with thirteen to twenty-five.

If you're not going to use something that exists as a foundation, determine from the beginning how many different items you want in your system. Typically, I suggest at least twenty-five to allow for some diversity in the readings. For example, if you're going to want thirty different symbols for your divinatory tool, then you'll need a medium that allows for that much variety. To illustrate, M&Ms have a limited number of colors, so they might not work here unless you consider their numeric value too!

What base material do you want to use (the medium)? You want your divination system to last a while (and I tend to eat the M&Ms too quickly), so keep that in mind. In particular, buttons, stones, dyed rice, metal rods, waxed leaves, and pressed flowers, small toys or charms, colored beans, jellybeans, and even coupons all make a perfectly good foundation. The only problem here is making sure whatever medium you choose offers enough symbolism to fit the pattern you chose in step one.

Do you want to lay this out like a tarot deck, pull the items, or cast the items? In casting systems, your symbols need not be the same size and shape, so this is ideal for things like animal figurines, unmatched stones, a variety of seashells, etc. Drawn systems, by comparison, must have objects of similar size and shape (like runes) so that you cannot recognize them when you touch them in the bag. Why? Even if you're not trying, knowing which is which can subconsciously skew your reading.

Will your system have upright and reversed meanings? The tarot is an example of a system that has both. Some readers, however, choose only to read the cards as upright, no matter how they're laid out. The advantage of reversed interpretations is that they offer insights into negatives, obstacles, reversals, and other things that may be influencing your question.

Pick out and detail the meaning of each one of the symbols in your divination kit. For example, say you've chosen to create a set of twenty-one stones. If this is a drawn or laid-out system, you'll need to find twenty-one stones of a similar size and shape. Once you get them, you need to determine what each one is going to mean, not only by itself but also in relationship to the other stones. In this case, you might look to the folkloric and metaphysical correspondences for the stones.

Last but not least, write down how the meanings of the items in your kit may change according to where they show up in a reading. For example, let's say you're using rose quartz to indicate self-confidence and appreciation, and that stone lands in a position that you've designated as an underlying influence. In this position, it could either mean that the answer to your question is being influenced by a lack of self-confidence or too much of it!

You can have as many positions in a reading as you wish, but they cannot exceed the total number of symbols in your kit. Here's a list of some of the possible positions your kit might have:

- Past
- Present
- Situation
- Obstacles
- Action called for
- Future
- Helpful influence
- Your environment
- Outcome
- Underlying circumstances
- Harmful influence
- Hopes and fears

If going through all this seems like a lot of work—it is, but it's worth it. In the end, you'll have a completely personalized and truly meaningful divination system. You'll already be familiar with the symbols you put into it, and you'll know exactly how to read it because of the thought that went into the creation process.

Using Divination Systems

By this point, you've hopefully made or found a divination system that you really like. The next step is actually using it. No need to have it sitting somewhere collecting dust when it could be providing you with valuable insights.

The first step here is to bless and charge your system just as you learned to do with spell components. Next, check yourself. If you feel the need to meditate, pray, or breathe to get yourself centered and completely in the moment, take the time to do just that. Divination is a type of magic that really relies on your ability to focus and let both energy and insights flow.

As you look through the reading, try to leave yourself open to Spirit's small voice. Many times, the reading will reveal things that you didn't ask about but really need to know. Other times, the meaning of the symbols shifts slightly—this happens for any number of reasons, including your own ability to see beyond the "system" and really touch on those things we cannot see but feel.

If you're doing a reading for yourself, you may find writing down the information and returning to it in an hour or so helps. Sometimes, we're too close to a specific question to get any type of perspective. If you're feeling uneasy or anxious about your question, those feelings can also alter the reading, making it inaccurate. That's why it's often good to find a friend who also enjoys divination and with whom you could trade readings. Your friend won't be quite so caught up in your questions and can provide more detached readings.

When you're reading for someone else, make sure you're not putting your own spin on the information you receive. For example, if someone asks about a relationship and you've just had a nasty breakup, it's human nature to see some of that negativity in the reading. But to be responsible to the person who's come to you for help—you cannot do that. Always try to be a positive prophet; never leave people feeling helpless or hopeless.

Speaking of which, what exactly should someone do with the information from a reading? First, always remember that life is what you make of it. No matter how a reading comes out, it's up to you to determine where, when, and how to apply that information (if at all). Any reader, including you, can be fallible and prone to adding in personal perspectives or prejudices. Therefore, it's very important that you keep this information in balance. It's not carved in stone, so trust your gut instincts. I've generally found that truth, if it's really "truth" for your life, returns again and again through unrelated sources. So, even if you toss out a piece of information that you should have actually paid attention to, you'll hear or read it in the future elsewhere.

Second, if you feel the reading you got was helpful with its perspectives, act on that information. It amazes me how many times people will come for a reading and when I look at the results I can see that they've already been told the same thing several times. In this case, typically that person is hoping someone will say something different—what they want to hear rather than what they need to hear. While that's a fairly normal avoidance response, it's not healthy. If you're not willing to act on new perspectives and begin internalizing changes, why bother going for a reading at all? It seems like a waste of good time to me.

Last but not least, take good care of your divination kit. After every reading, take a minute to cleanse the items in your system (using incense, lemon water, or whatever else works for you). Also, find a safe place to keep the kit when it's not in use. Many people like little wooden boxes or lined pouches for this purpose. These types of containers serve two functions: they keep people and pets from randomly tinkering with your tools, and they also help divert unwanted energies so the system is always at its best and ready for your use.

Give it a Try!

With all the technicalities out of the way, you're probably very eager to try some divination methods. I've assembled a few user-friendly systems here that I think you'll find work pretty well no matter how experienced you are with divination. Try them out, adapt them, or use them as a jumping-off point for making a system of your own.

By the Numbers

Numerology has a long history most readily traceable to Pythagoras (circa 500 BCE) who believed in the mystical nature of numbers. That belief has not waned over the years. In fact, spells often utilize numeric symbolism, and numerology is still used by many Neo-Pagans when considering where to move (the house number), propitious dates for an event, and so forth.

To determine a personality number (which reveals the overall attributes of yourself or another person), you add together the month, day, and year of your birth. So, February 21, 1960, translates into 2 + 2 + 1 + 1 + 9 + 6 + 0 = 21. Twenty-one becomes 2 + 1 = 3. Note that using this system also works to determine how good a choice you're making in planning a date for something specific (like a ritual). You just add together the numbers of the date, month, and year of the event in question, then review the associations below for insights.

To determine a birth number, use the chart below according to your full name given at birth. Add up all the numbers as with the personality number until you reach a single-digit sum. This number indicates habits and traits. Adding up only the vowels in your name shows your inner self.

Here is a list of the basic interpretations for the numbers 1 through 9:

1. **A, J, S.** A high-energy person or situation with lots of creative value, but little regulation or fore-

thought. You need ambition and self-assurance to meet this type of individual or circumstance head-on.

2. **B, K, T.** A sensitive, diplomatic person or situation where there's a lot of balance and equity. Good communication skills and the ability to socialize will help you here.
3. **C, L, U.** An inventive, flexible person or situation where appearance counts for a lot. Your ability to remain independent and proactive is the key to success with individuals or circumstances that bear this number.
4. **D, M, V.** A logical, practical person or situation where everything proceeds in a very orderly manner. You will need to be able to make friends easily and show great loyalty or have strong research skills if this number comes up.
5. **E, N, W.** An impulsive or adventurous person or situation where intensity and pleasure are central. You'll need to be able to adapt to fast changes or possibly take on a leadership role when the sum is 5.
6. **F, O, X.** A loving, artsy, and beauty-oriented job, situation, or person where caring about individuals and trust are highly valued attributes. You'll need to be willing to show approval and provide support in interacting with this number.
7. **G, P, Y.** A philosophical, intuitive situation or person filled with mystery and curiosity. Number 7 values a strong sense of discipline, intelligence, and has uncanny luck.
8. **H, Q, Z.** A variable situation or person, prone to rapid changes from great success to great failure.

You'll need to have a strong sense of self and overcome the 8's tendency to be a wallflower for success with this number.
9. **I, R.** A situation or person that brings out the warrior spirit, bravery, and an amazing work ethic. Nines have a harsh temper that needs to be balanced with calm insight.

Pay particular attention to any number that keeps coming up in these calculations or other mundane situations. This means that number has some type of strong influence, and it can show hidden potentials or things to avoid. For example, before signing up for a specific class, compare the teacher's name to your own, using numerology to see how well you'll get along with them.

Candles

Divination by candles (formally called *lychnomancy* or *pyromancy*) has been around for nearly as long as the candle itself. Since the candle was once a common household object, it's not surprising that people used it in magic too. Often, the color of the candle is dictated by the theme of their question, such as yellow for business, green for money, and red for love.

The basic procedure for candle divination is very simple. Focus on your question, light the candle, then observe the movement of the flames. Your results can be interpreted as follows:

- **Candle Refuses to Light:** Something's wrong. Your plans may not be well thought out. Alternatively, this is a no response to a yes or no question.

- **Burns Dimly:** Move slowly. Don't make any fast decisions.
- **Bright Flames:** This is a positive response—move ahead with confidence.
- **Dancing Flames:** There will be a lot of movement and change ahead.
- **Split Flame:** This represents a crossroads or division of opinions.
- **Sparking Flame:** Heated feelings, anger, and some type of news are on the horizon.
- **Wax Dripping Down the Left Side:** This is a negative sign for relationships.
- **Brilliant, Tall Flame:** This represents good luck.
- **Candle Goes Out:** Bad news is forthcoming.

Another way to use your candle for divination is to think of a question while holding the candle sideways over a bowl of cold water. Keep focusing on the question, allowing the wax to drip into the water and solidify for about one minute. You can interpret the resulting shapes much as you would an inkblot. For example, a key shape might mean an opening of some sort or an opportunity. A heart has to do with matters of love (is it whole or broken?), a house speaks of family matters or a possible move, and so forth. If you like the results you get from wax drippings, you can carry them as a portable charm to help manifest that energy!

Just one word of caution—please do not let candle wax go down your drains. It will clog the sinks and make your parents quite hesitant to let you use candles in the future. Also, take normal precautions to ensure fire safety wherever you're working (I hear that burning witches is quite passé, let's keep it that way).

Dowsing

There are a variety of types of dowsing (the use of wands, rods, twigs, or pendulums to discover information). For the sake of simplicity, we'll cover two of the most common types I've seen—namely "water witching" and pendulum work. Let's start with water witching.

Dowsing Rods
While there were all types of wands and rods used for magical purposes earlier in history, it was around the 1400s that dowsing with wooden wands gained popularity. At this juncture, the wands were used for finding ore, water, property lines, lost domestic animals, and even the four directions. Today, they're used similarly to find energy lines (also called "lay lines") or to help in locating lost items.

To try dowsing with a wooden wand, you'll need a fallen branch (fourteen to eighteen inches in length) that's shaped like a Y. If the branch is peach, dogwood, hazel, mulberry, juniper, maple, or willow, all the better. Hold the forked end of the branch in each hand with the long part of the branch running parallel to the ground. When the branch dips downward, that marks a spot to check. The theory here is that your inner witch basically becomes a psychic sonograph, with the wooden branch being the needle to pinpoint energy or items.

Some witchcraft shops now sell dowsing kits made from two L-shaped metal rods. To use this system, you hold the short end, one in each hand, and walk the area. When the two wands cross, that's considered a hit. You should always repeat the process a couple of times for confirmation, remembering to focus on the item or energies you are seeking.

Pendulum

Romans were perhaps the first people to use pendulums, but they appeared in a variety of cultural settings. For our purposes, it's a different form of dowsing that uses a pointed crystal on a chain or string. Sometimes, a bundle of herbs, a leaf, a flower, or a ring can be used as a substitute. The only real problem with pendulums is the fact that they provide a limited amount of information, typically answering yes or no with little clarification.

To try pendulum work, just take a ring (without a stone) and suspend it on a long string. Now, put your elbow down on a table and hold the free end of the string between the thumb and index finger of your strong hand. The pendulum should be about two inches above the table or the palm of your other hand (adjust the string accordingly). Make sure the pendulum is still before you start.

Next, concentrate on a simple yes or no question. Watch for any movements in the ring. An up-down (forward/back) movement means yes, happiness, or good news. A side-to-side movement (left/right) means no, slow down, or stop. Just getting this much of an answer may take you several tries, so don't get discouraged. If the ring just twirls in a circle or bobs, it means there's currently no answer, a great deal of uncertainty, or conflict regarding the question.

Once you get a little bit more confident you can start looking for more subtle information. Ellipses, for example, reveal a lack of clear understanding or communication or two equally interesting options. If they move east to west, this typically reveals itself in a relationship. If they move north to south, you need to depend more heavily on your instincts. If they move diagonally, take care that the ethics and information you're getting are both on the up-and-up.

You can change the color of your string to indicate the theme of your question. You can also change what you attach to the string to better indicate the purpose of the endeavor. For example, you could attach a rosebud to a pink string for a question about a relationship.

Dream Work

Did you ever wake up with the feeling that what you saw during your sleep was important, that there was a message in your dream to which you should pay attention? You're not alone. In fact, dream interpretation was and still is a favorite hobby for a lot of people. The Greeks and Egyptians both valued dreams for what they could reveal about everyday life, and even about the future. So do modern witches!

When you sleep the barriers that normally divide the conscious from the unconscious mind are opened. This allows all kinds of images to seep into dreams. Some of these images come from the media, some come from daily activities, some are from memories, and some can be inspired by the pizza and soda you had earlier! And for those of you who are saying "but I don't dream" — that's not true! Everyone dreams, it's just that we don't always wake up at the right time to remember the details.

So, how can you use your dreams as a mode of divination? Well, you may not have to do anything special. Dreams already communicate a lot of information about daily circumstances to us, and sometimes even things about which we may be unaware. However, if you want to encourage psychic dreams that really get to the heart of a question, here are some steps you can take to encourage them:

- Meditate before you go to sleep. As you sit quietly, repeat whatever question you have over and over, either out loud or mentally.
- Pray for an insightful dream (you can call on your Patron/ness or a Spirit guide for assistance).
- Use jasmine, marigold, rose, or balsam in incense, teas, or oils to encourage psychic dreams.
- Keep an amethyst or azurite under your pillow (both are very strong dreaming stones).
- Bask in the light of a full moon. This charges your intuitive nature.
- Make sure that you have a tape recorder or pen and paper handy. Write down any memories of your dreams as soon as you wake up (these tend to fade the longer you wait).

The next obvious question becomes, how can you tell what dreams are important and which ones were just the result of indigestion? First off, if the dream seems to focus on a personal fantasy, a memory, or just normal daily clutter, it's probably not spiritually significant. However, if your question pertained to something more mundane, take a close look at it anyway.

There are typically three signs of an important dream. First, it's very vivid to the point where you don't realize you're dreaming until you wake up. Second, you may find you have difficulty shaking the dream—the images come back to you all day long, unlike other dreams that just fade away. Third, if you've recorded the dream, rereading it may bring up unexpected reactions—emotions or even physical feelings.

When you have this type of dream the next step is to consider what it means to you or to your question. Sometimes a dream is very obvious because of what's happening in your life. These dreams don't really need to be picked apart (don't over-spiritualize—sometimes a rock is just a rock). When the meaning is less obvious, however, you can use this guideline to find clues in the dream:

- As previously mentioned, write down the dream or tape-record it in as much detail as possible as soon as possible.
- After several hours, re-read the dream. If anything else comes back to you, add it to your original notes.
- Look for the lowest common denominator in the dream—for example, if a dog is running, water is running, and an electrical line is running, the key is *running*.
- Look for repeated symbols, be it a color, number, emblem, etc.
- Consider patterns, cycles, and progressions in the dream (especially those that seem to mirror real life).
- Check for folklore, sayings, cultural influences, and even puns that may be appearing. (Both our minds and spirits have a sense of humor.)
- If you find you're having trouble expressing the dream in words, consider using other artistic mediums— perhaps sing or paint your dream.

After coming up with a list of central images and themes based on the above, you can look them up in a good dream dictionary. Remember that dream interpretation is very subjective. What your dream means to you and what it means to someone else will be very different. Ultimately, what it means to you is most important, so always trust your first instincts.

Fruity, Flavorful Insights

Being a kitchen witch, I love to create magical methods that are not only fun but edible. For this activity, you need nothing more than a can of fruit salad (the more variety in the fruit, the better). Of course, you can make a fruit salad from scratch if that appeals to you. In any case, put the fruit salad into a bowl and stir it clockwise while you think of a question. If possible, repeat the question out loud four times. Now close your eyes, dip in a spoon, and, using this basic interpretive guide, see what answer you've served up for yourself:

- **Apple:** finding a healthy solution to a problem or a relationship. It is also a sign of love and peace.
- **Banana:** a focus on spiritual matters, especially the need for protection. Also indicates forthcoming luck.
- **Blackberry:** positive results will come from your efforts.
- **Blueberry:** an omen for happiness. Alternatively, indicates the need to be more safety minded.
- **Cherry:** a very positive omen for relationships, especially romantic relationships.
- **Date:** abundant results can be expected from your endeavors.
- **Fig:** the need for physical strength. Focus on the material/mundane world right now.
- **Grape (or raisin):** pay attention to your dreams. They're trying to tell you something.
- **Grapefruit:** clean out the old and welcome the new. Leave the past behind.
- **Lemon:** pay attention to your health. Alternatively, this may refer to some type of positive change in a relationship.

- **Lime:** clean up your act. Work on ridding yourself of bad habits.
- **Mango:** take more time to meditate and give yourself downtime.
- **Melon:** this is a good sign for a serious relationship.
- **Mulberry:** growth in your psychic awareness.
- **Orange:** a sign of happiness and improved financial flow.
- **Peach:** be sure you're making a wise choice.
- **Pear:** whatever you're working on will have long-lasting results.
- **Pineapple:** you'll be welcome wherever you go.
- **Plum:** stay away from negative people and situations.
- **Pomegranate:** depend on your creativity to help you with this question.
- **Raspberry:** cheer up! Things aren't as bad as they may seem.
- **Strawberry:** love is in your future.
- **Watermelon:** take good care of your health.

By the way, you can do something similar with vegetables if you wish. Use a book, like my *Kitchen Witch's Cookbook,* to help discern the traditional magical associations for various foods.

The Grab-Bag

This method works best for simple questions that don't require a lot of detail, but it's a lot of fun. Think of a question. Get it clearly in your mind. Then reach into your backpack and, with your eyes closed, randomly pull out the first thing that comes into your hand. You can interpret the results using this list as a starting point:

- **A Black Item:** a negative (or no) answer.
- **A Red Item:** stop whatever you're doing and wait.
- **A Yellow Item:** be cautious.
- **A Green Item:** a positive (or yes) response.
- **A White Item:** what are your real intentions here?
- **A Blue Item:** if it will really make you happy, go for it.
- **A Purple Item:** consider this for a while before you do or say anything.
- **A Pencil:** communications are at the heart of your question, but you can fix the problem.
- **A Pen:** another communication problem, but this one is much harder to repair. Make sure what you're saying and meaning is what's being heard.
- **An Eraser:** oops! You've messed up somehow, so go clean it up.
- **A Notebook:** pay attention. There's something you're missing here.
- **A Ruler:** measure your decision carefully in your heart and your head.
- **A Paper Clip:** what connections have you been missing?

Feel free to add items to this list with your own interpretations for greater variety. By the way, if you happen to grab a book, consider the title of that book as part of your answer. For example, your math textbook could indicate that something in this situation doesn't quite "add up" and you need more information. Or, if you grabbed a chemistry book, consider what's happening between you and other people—is the chemistry working?

Mirror, Mirror

Divination by mirrors is called *catoptromancy*. It's believed that the art originated in Persia or China and later found its way into Greece, Rome, India, and Tibet. The type of surface used varied from polished obsidian to an actual mirrored surface, and magical mirrors were typically made during special times with very precise ingredients. Thankfully, it's much easier to make one of your own today.

To make a scrying mirror, begin with a simple framed mirror or frame with a glass panel of any size. Apply a coat of black paint to the surface of the mirror. While that's drying, I like to sprinkle a little fairy dust (finely powdered opalescent glitter) into the paint. This seems to help people who have trouble with visualization or scrying because it gives your eyes something on which to focus. Once it dries, add a clear protective coat so the paint won't fleck off easily.

Once that's dry, return the mirror to its frame with the black side out. Sit down with the mirror at eye level, with a lit candle near the front right or left of it. If possible, dim the lights in the room and focus your attention on the mirror's surface. Let your vision go a little blurry (this happens pretty naturally) and keep watching while you think of a question.

What each person sees can be very different. Some actually see images (literal or symbolic), while others see moving veils or clouds. If you see images, make a note of them and look them up in a dream dictionary or other symbol guide. If you see moving veils or clouds, you can use this list to help you interpret the reading:

- **Movement left or down:** negative, declining energies (a no).
- **Movement right or up:** positive, growing energies (a yes).
- **Reddish veils, wisps, or clouds:** be careful and cautious, there may be danger.
- **Yellow veils, wisps, or clouds:** improved energy and inventiveness; good times ahead.
- **Purple veils, wisps, or clouds:** focus on your spirituality or path.
- **Green veils, wisps, or clouds:** slow, steady progress.
- **Blue veils, wisps, or clouds:** take a break from everything and relax.
- **Orange veils, wisps, or clouds:** solid efforts will yield results.

If two or more colors appear, blend the interpretations together. For example, if you see orange and green it means that you'll make progress, but it will be slow and measured.

Be patient with yourself. Scrying is difficult for many people, and it takes time to get good at it. With practice however, you'll find that you'll get more detailed results.

Monopoly Magic

This is a good example of a casting system. You're going to need a collection of various game tokens. In looking through things at my house, I found the figure of a person, house, die, car, ladder, coin, and shoe. These are the tokens I'll use for example interpretations here, but you're likely to find other tokens, and you'll want to determine their interpretations yourself. Again, trust yourself.

- **Person figurine:** an influential individual.
- **House:** your focus is on the wrong place—look to home.
- **Die:** odd coincidences and bits of luck abound.
- **Car:** travel or movement.
- **Ladder:** upward movement, improvements.
- **Coin:** spending money perhaps more than you should have.
- **Shoe:** the need to improve your foundations (keep one foot on the ground).

Next, get a large piece of construction paper (or cut open a grocery bag) and draw a circle on it. Divide the circle into twelve sections, numbered one to twelve.

This is the surface on which you'll cast your tokens. Where the token lands determines which area of your life it applies to, as follows:

1. The present—important pressing matters
2. Relationships
3. School
4. Travel or adventure
5. Family and home
6. Money or legal matters
7. Conscious issues
8. Intuitive issues
9. Body (health)
10. Friends
11. Problems or obstacles to overcome
12. The future

Putting this together, you'd put your tokens in a small pouch, hold them a moment, then scatter them on the surface by opening the pouch and turning it over. For the sake of illustration, let's say the person token landed in position 3, the car on 4, the house on 10, the die, coin, and ladder on 6, and the shoe on 7. This might be interpreted as follows:

There is an influential person at school who can help you achieve your goals. Seek them out. You have some nice adventure coming up, perhaps a field trip or vacation with your family. Know that your family offers you support and friendship even when other people may leave you hanging.

The coin, ladder and die on six implies a really good change of pace financially. Perhaps you're about to land that after-school job you've been wanting or find another way to make some "fun" money. Finally, with the shoe on 7, you need to be aware that you tend to dream a little too much. Redirect your attention to daily matters and stay focused.

As you can see, this system offers a lot of room for personalization and expansion. Just find more tokens!

Pets' Paws

If you own a cat or dog, folk traditions tell us that watching them can give you clues about what's to come. It's thought that this particular tradition (at least with cats) began in Egypt where they were worshipped. Here's a list of behaviors for which to watch:

Cats
- **Cat washing face:** visitors are coming—prepare!
- **Cat cleaning itself in the doorway:** a minister is going to call you or come over.
- **Cat washing its ear:** be prepared for a change in the weather.

- **Cat leaving your house:** leave with it—this is a bad sign.
- **Stray cat being taken in:** a very good sign, much luck ahead.
- **Calico cat sighted in random location:** very good fortune for a new project.
- **Black cat walking across the road:** make a wish. It might come true.
- **Cat entering the room right paw first:** if you've just asked a question, the answer is yes.

Dogs
- **Dog howling:** beware of any partnership you're considering.
- **Dog entering your house and lying on the bed immediately:** you'll soon be getting some new items (perhaps as gifts).
- **Black dog crossing your path:** be very careful—bad luck is close at hand.
- **Dog howling at midnight:** some type of ending.
- **Dog rolling around on the ground or hiding under the table:** a thunderstorm is coming.

Play Your Hand (Cards, That Is)

Another wonderfully inexpensive form of divination, all you need is a normal set of playing cards. Our modern decks are actually descended from the tarot, each suit relating to the four suits of the Minor Arcana (clubs = rods and pertain to mundane matters like business; hearts = cups and deal with our emotions; diamonds = coins and deal with finances; and spades = swords and represent challenges).

The only caution I would issue is that, just because these are ordinary playing cards, doesn't mean you should treat them any differently from any other magical tool. Once you use them for divination, they've taken on a spiritual context and should be respected. In fact, you may even want to keep a separate deck just for divination to stress that level of respect.

To use the deck, you can follow any tarot layout to configure the pattern and progression of your reading. Reversed cards imply a lessening of the interpretation or a contrary meaning. Here's a list of common interpretations:

Clubs
- **Ace:** improved finances and joy
- **King:** a kind, masculine individual who is very direct, yet willing to listen
- **Queen:** a feminine individual who's very generous and romantic
- **Jack:** a young person with a lot of wisdom and energy
- **Ten:** success or victory
- **Nine:** an unexpected victory or streak of luck
- **Eight:** gifts from another person help you greatly
- **Seven:** catching up to and possibly surpassing a goal
- **Six:** success and prosperity
- **Five:** an unexpected social outlet is forthcoming
- **Four:** prepare for some type of failure or disappointment
- **Three:** anger or frustrations get resolved
- **Two:** be very careful with your resources

Hearts
- **Ace:** good news is coming
- **King:** a very open-minded masculine individual
- **Queen:** a compassionate and feminine individual who has a strong presence
- **Jack:** a young person who loves adventure

- **Ten:** success, even when the odds are against you
- **Nine:** your unspoken wish or desire comes true
- **Eight:** friendship or gentle affection returned
- **Seven:** improved relationships and peaceful resolutions
- **Six:** don't give up, things are just about to get better
- **Five:** listen to advice from someone you trust
- **Four:** you may be moving or making another change soon
- **Three:** prepare for rough waters
- **Two:** a new friend or financial improvements (or both!)

Spades
- **Ace:** a pleasurable time or focus on pleasure
- **King:** a masculine individual who isn't telling you the truth or who harbors jealousy
- **Queen:** a single and feminine individual who is very loving
- **Jack:** a young person who has no common sense or manners and often plots against others (typically practical jokes)
- **Ten:** sadness or depression brought about by unexpected news
- **Nine:** a very bad announcement or a streak of really bad luck
- **Eight:** whatever you're planning will not take place
- **Seven:** a bump in the road—try to clear up the misunderstanding
- **Six:** a turnaround (for better or worse)
- **Five:** friends aid and provide relief and understanding
- **Four:** difficulties with a job or a relationship
- **Three:** some type of ending or separation
- **Two:** purposeful lies that are very harmful

Diamonds
- **Ace:** get outdoors and have some fun
- **King:** a masculine individual who has a very short temper, to the point of being dangerous
- **Queen:** a feminine individual who always gossips and spreads rumors
- **Jack:** a young person who deceives everyone
- **Ten:** transitions or a move
- **Nine:** lots of red tape—nothing happens quickly now
- **Eight:** a new or refreshed romance
- **Seven:** take some time out to find peace in your heart
- **Six:** renewed physical, mental, or spiritual health
- **Five:** financial victory or advancement at work
- **Four:** improvements are on the horizon
- **Three:** watch for legal troubles
- **Two:** a new pet project or relationship that you really love

Sets of Adjacent Face Cards
- **Four aces:** potential failure—watch your work
- **Three aces:** great news
- **Two aces:** someone is trying to undermine you
- **Four kings:** victory and a well-deserved honor
- **Three kings:** pay attention to important advice (often from a masculine individual)
- **Two kings:** a new friendship or partnership
- **Four queens:** social occasions
- **Three queens:** an odd letter or phone call
- **Two queens:** seeing old friends or family members
- **Four jacks:** a group of young people (friends)
- **Three jacks:** people pretending to be friends but with hidden motives
- **Two jacks:** something's wrong; you're not seeing the whole picture

Rock Readings

Earlier in this chapter, I talked about the stone system that I put together for myself. You may enjoy making a similar casting collection for personal use. First, you need to pick out at least thirteen different stones. Since this set is cast, they need not be the same size and shape. In fact, having both pointed and round stones helps with the reading because the pointed stones act like arrows, drawing your attention to another stone.

Next, determine the meanings of each stone you've chosen. Here's a list of the stones I use and how I interpret them:

- **Botswana Agate (pink and gray):** In a positive position, it reveals that bravery, love, and kindness are the keys to success. In a negative position, it symbolizes being untrue to yourself or that someone is lying to you.
- **Mexican Agate (brown, white, and red):** Stay true to your path and don't lose hope. Alternatively, you are seeking too much external teaching that isn't being internalized or applied.
- **Amethyst:** In a positive position, improved peace, self-control, and overcoming blockages. Alternatively, being anxious, depressed, or jumping too quickly into a situation.
- **Aventurine (dark green with gold flecks):** A bit of good luck will come your way. Alternatively, technical troubles abound. Nothing's going to move quickly right now.
- **Bloodstone (green with red flecks):** Improved health, success in a battle, or fitting in with a new group. Alternatively, blockage, frustration, and awkwardness in social situations.

- **Carnelian:** Feelings of happiness and joy. Your patience finally returns. Alternatively, foreboding, not feeling appreciated, jealousy.
- **Fluorite:** The positive application of personal skills brings fulfillment—trust yourself! Alternatively, scattering your energy in too many places—get some focus.
- **Obsidian:** In a positive position, problems are working out positively (usually with friends or family). Alternatively, giving in to your emotions without thinking things through. Be aware of those things you cannot change and let them go.
- **Pāua shell:** Positively, resistance finally wears away and opportunity knocks. Alternatively, be wary of taking advice from someone—they may have a hidden agenda.
- **Quartz (clear):** Mental clarity and strength; renewed energy. Alternatively, you are not standing up for something you know is right and just.
- **Quartz (rose):** A new friendship or improved appreciation of self. Alternatively, could reflect stormy relationships and distraction.
- **Quartz (snow):** In a positive position, you have been given a chance to rest and relax—take it! Alternatively, you are not paying attention to your own needs. Refill the inner well or you'll continue to feel disjointed and restless.
- **Sodalite (dark blue with white flecks):** A period of anger, guilt, or stress finally ends. Alternatively, problems loom on the horizon, often those that come from not listening to your instincts.
- **Tiger's-eye:** The shadows of the past are chased away by the hope of a new project or partner. You have the courage and energy to face anything head-on. Alternatively, you want to retreat from life but have nowhere to hide.

- **Unakite (green and pink):** If you've considered a new project, now is the time to act—your creativity is flowing! Alternatively, procrastination leads to problems. You have to stop dancing on the fence and act.

Besides the stones, you'll also need a cloth napkin that you can write on with a permanent marker. Any color napkin is fine, but yellow is a good choice since that's the color associated with divinatory skills. Also, try to find one that's made of natural fibers like cotton or linen.

Lay the napkin out so that it makes a diamond shape in front of you. Mark the upper corner with "North/Winter," the right corner with "East/Spring," the lower corner with "South/Summer," and the left corner with "West/Fall." The center of the napkin gets labeled "Self/Now." If you wish, around the edge of the entire napkin write the words the future.

Think of your question while holding the stones in your hand, then release them onto the cloth. Here's how these positions affect the way you read the stones that land in those regions in your casting:

- **Self/Now:** You today. Circumstances as they exist. Very personal matters.
- **North/Winter:** Things that are slow or at a standstill. Use this time to tend the seeds of your dreams and wait until spring.
- **East/Spring:** Wishes that are starting to manifest. New beginnings. Excelling in your studies.
- **South/Summer:** Social activity, change, and other fiery feelings (including negative ones, like anger) are all stressed by this region.

- **West/Water:** The seeds you planted are finally maturing for the harvest. Emotions are overemphasized here, and money may be tight. Trust the voice of wisdom.

Let's put this into an example using one "stone," the Pāua shell, so you get a feel for how to interpret your castings. If this landed on the Self/Now position, I'd say you need to heed your own inner voice on your question and be very diligent in pursuing your goal. If it landed on the North position, it seems like your question is going to take time to work out, and that some of the advice you're getting isn't good.

On the East position, it symbolizes a great start for something that's very meaningful to you, just be careful that you're not being so rigid that you miss other good opportunities here. On the South position, Pāua talks of an argument that arose out of council you received that wasn't appreciated or that had bad motivations at the outset. Finally, on the West position, this shell implies insightful abilities that surprise you and help greatly in answering this question. Now is not the time to give up but, rather, look within!

Hopefully, this chapter has given you all kinds of ideas for making or adapting divination systems. As you've seen, there are no limits as to what items you might use to improve your insight and strengthen your inner psychic. However, there is one other thing that can and will help you develop into a more adept witch—namely, ritual work. This is something that works cooperatively with your spells and divinations if you wish to combine them.

Chapter VII

Bedroom Feng Shui

Of all the rooms in your home, your bedroom is probably the most special to you. This is where you can simply be without judgment, nagging, or discussions. This is where you can listen to your music, daydream, or play around on the computer, and it's also where you can mull over your magical path and future without siblings, parents, or even pets interrupting you every five minutes. That's why I've chosen to focus on this space (or any other area you use when you want real privacy) for this chapter.

As you continually interact with your personal space, it can have a huge influence on the quality of your life, both consciously and subconsciously. This space reflects the true you both inwardly and outwardly. It's where you regenerate, heal, sort through your feelings, and it is the one spot where you can, hopefully, find peace. Sadly, we're not usually taught to connect with our environments, nor are we typically made aware of the impact they may have. Living and working spaces that are out of balance or blocked make for daily lives that are similarly out of sorts. In contrast, when we begin to connect and truly understand our space (including our bodies), it makes for a far healthier and happier existence.

That's where feng shui comes in. Feng shui is quite simply the art of mindful placement. It's based on the idea that just as people have an energy field, every item and structure has its own unique energy pattern (like a fingerprint). That pattern, since you live within it, constantly interacts with your life's situations. Thus, the intent of feng shui is to purposefully align everything from knickknacks to whole homes so that each re-establishes or inspires a positive flow of energy (called chi).

The best way to think of chi is as "good vibrations." Chi is already a part of all living things. The key is learning to recognize it and direct it effectively, even as you're learning to recognize and direct your magic. By doing so, you're promoting happiness, health, peace, and balance in your body, mind, and spirit (not to mention your living space).

The first step in this recognition process is to simply consider how various objects in your personal space make you feel. If an item brings up a bad memory, ask yourself if you really need it. If not, toss it out or give it away and replace it with something that has more uplifting imagery. If an item reminds you of the "old" you, any destructive behaviors you've been trying to overcome, or you're keeping it because you feel obligated to do so, seriously consider getting rid of this negative clutter. Finally, if an item is lying around just taking up space, it can block positive chi, which, in turn, can cause a lot of issues in your life to remain in a holding pattern—so pick it up and put it away. Finally, a good reason to keep your room clean!

Ancient Chinese Secret

If you're not a big history buff, you can skip this section, but I've always felt that to use a system effectively, one should first understand a bit of where it came from.

By understanding these roots, you can then respectfully adapt and apply the original concepts to modern reality, specifically your reality.

The roots of feng shui are very long and a bit tangled. In China, this practical philosophy has existed for thousands of years. At the beginning of the Chou dynasty (1122–207 BCE), a system called the *Pa-K'ua* began being utilized by King Wen. The Pa-K'ua consists of eight trigrams, each of which corresponds to a point on the compass. These are used to describe patterns of change in the natural world. By the eighth century BCE, the Pa-K'ua and the theory of change were combined to promote the flow of chi inside a city or a palace.

Around 206–219 BCE, the art of *K'an-Yu* (the study of the energy carried in landforms) was added to Pa-K'ua. The philosophy of K'an-Yu stated that the land's energy could dramatically affect a person or a whole country. Come the Chin dynasty (265–420 CE), everyday citizens started using K'an-Yu in choosing sites for houses and burial grounds (Yin-domain feng shui.) By 600 CE, the tombs of royal families were created in strict adherence to feng shui guidelines. Here is a brief historical outline of feng shui:

- **2000–1700 BCE:** People use astrology and auspicious timing to assist in moving or finding a divination site.
- **1700–1027 BCE:** Writing invented, sundial used to track time, and oracle bone divination practiced.
- **960 BCE:** Recorded theories of Feng Shui written down for the first time.
- **770–476 BCE:** Confucius and Lao Zi born, the I Ching (a foundation to feng shui) written.
- **221–207 BCE:** The first feng shui classic, *Green Satchel,* written.

- **25 CE:** The theories of feng shui translated into principles more closely resembling those we use today.
- **265–316 CE:** *The Book of Burial* by Guo Pu discusses using feng shui to change a person's fate.
- **589–960 CE:** Feng shui theory becomes current fashion in practice.
- **960–1368 CE:** East-West system of feng shui develops.

The United States was first introduced to feng shui during the California gold rush of the mid-1800s, when many were seeking their fortunes. Though the Chinese had brought their beliefs in feng shui principles to this country, they were foreign and difficult for the early Californians to understand and accept. Now, 150 years later, feng shui is being reintroduced to the West. The main system utilized is the one based on the compass, as opposed to land masses (which are kind of hard to work with in your bedroom).

Compass Style Feng Shui for Magic

Feng shui is an excellent source of potential energy, especially in terms of where you place charms, amulets, and other sacred objects in your room, home, or other sacred space. Because chi works with eight regions (directions), combining this system with your magic is very easy since Neo-Wiccans use the four quarters already. This just gives you more variety to consider where you work a spell or ritual, or where you put symbolic objects/items in a room to encourage specific energies.

Compass Points and Energy Keynotes
- **North:** nurture and sustain life; motivating change

- **Northeast:** progress and prosperity; slow, gradual change
- **East:** beginnings and hope; quickening energy and motivation
- **Southeast:** caution and consistency; building energy wisely
- **South:** tenacity and zeal; fast transformations and flexibility
- **Southwest:** comfort and peace; calming energy and releasing stress
- **West:** balance and cool-headedness; smooth, flowing energy
- **Northwest:** self-extension and empowerment; expanding energy

To understand this and use it successfully, you'll first need to review the correspondences for each direction of a space, room, or home, beginning in the north (or the position of noon).

North
This region governs careers. In your case, this might apply to school or to whatever future work plans you have. Add highlights of blue and black to this region and fish tanks or images of water to improve the overall energy flow. When you're thinking about getting an after-school job, if you want a raise at a job you already have, or when you need to establish some harmony among the elements of your personal life, school, and work, consider enacting a spell in this part of your home or room. If you don't have time for that, put an item that represents your goal near this spot.

For example, if you're trying to get an after-school job, take the business card from the place to which you applied, wrap it in blue or black cloth, and place a change jar on top of it in (or near) the north. Add a magical element to this positioning by reciting some type of incantation like:

> *"Responsibility; I will not shirk,*
> *____ hours a day I wish to work,*
> *and as these coins gather and grow,*
> *into my life—money flows."*

Fill in the blank with the number of hours you can reasonably work and still fulfill your other daily obligations at home and school. Don't overextend yourself here.

If you're having trouble with your job or in a class that's focused on your future career, take a look at this part of your room and home very closely. If the space is cluttered or closed off, you're losing good chi flow. Open things up (including windows, curtains, and doors). If the weather is disagreeable, apply this concept symbolically by opening your closet door and leaving your drawers slightly ajar. As with the previous example, you can further support the symbolism by reciting an incantation such as:

> *"Open the way; open the flow,*
> *good vibes come in,*
> *bad vibes all go!"*

If you feel that out of respect for housemates or parents, you should not recite an incantation out loud, just recite it in your mind. Stay focused, and the effect will be the same.

Northeast

This is another area strongly connected with school in that it rules over matters of learning and the conscious mind. Highlight this area with shades of yellow and brown and keep living plants nearby to honor the Earth Element. When you find you're having trouble building solid spiritual foundations, when you're distracted easily by daydreams, or find you can't easily shake free from residual energy after a day's magic, this is an excellent area in which to meditate.

Sit on the ground (to physically emphasize that earth connection). Breathe deeply and visualize sparkling gold light pouring into your energetic body, moving from the top of your head into the earth below you. As it reaches your legs and feet, the light turns brown-colored and appears like roots to hold you secure. If you notice that you feel slightly heavier or that your center of gravity has shifted down toward your hips, you're doing the visualization correctly.

When you find your ability to concentrate at school is disrupted, this is a great place in which to study. Get a good light with a broad-spectrum bulb (this is like sunlight, and it stresses conscious awareness). Dab the bulb with a little rosemary oil (to improve your memory), and then get down to business. If you wish, you can recite an incantation before you begin four times (the number of Earth and foundations). Here's one example:

"My mind's been muddy,
Sunlight—help me to study,
By your powerful rays—distractions all fade,
By my will and with time,
good grades will be mine!"

If you can have a yellow candle burning nearby that will also encourage the energy you're trying to create (just remember to ask your parents' permission first). Alternatively, wear brown and/or yellow-colored clothing afterward to help you carry the energy you've created into school (especially for tests).

East

Feng shui tells us that this region influences matters of health and your overall family unit. As in Neo-Wicca, this is also a region filled with hope and new beginnings. Use highlights of sky blue and vibrant green here, along with any wooden items to support a positive energy flow toward these parts of your life.

In particular, work spells, rituals, and meditations in the East when you're starting a new project, when you or those in your family have had ongoing sicknesses you're coping with, or when you find the tension levels at home are reaching critical mass. I find that candle-burning efforts in this area are particularly symbolic and useful (since the East is where the sun's fire rises). Using the three situations noted:

- **New Project:** At dawn, light a pale blue candle in the eastern region of your home or room when starting a new project in order to put a fire under it. The color blue here will also provide you with a sense of inner peace regarding this effort.
- **Sickness:** Carve the name of the person who's ill into the candle. As you do, speak the name of the sickness into the carving. Light it just as the Sun comes over the horizon and let it burn down completely. The melting candle and the fire's purity help turn away

the energy of sickness. Warning: This should not be done in lieu of proper medical treatment.
- **Tension in the Home:** Any time during the day, take out a blue candle and carve it with a peace sign. Also, take out a black candle and name it "stress." Put these in the eastern section of your home/room. Light the black candle and focus all your negativity into it. Next, take the blue candle and place the top of it upside down on the black candle's flame so that the blue is lit but puts out the black one completely. Symbolically, this represents peace being born from anxiety (and overcoming the darkness). If possible, let the candle burn for at least four hours to establish the energy.

During the last two processes, you may want to add smoke cleansing to clear out any residual energies that could negatively impact health and well-being. Typically, suffumigation wands are made from sage, cedar, lavender, and/or sweetgrass. Choose one that won't bother folks with allergies. Light it and move clockwise around your space, starting and ending in the East. Visualize bright, white-blue light pouring out of the smoke into every part of the home.

Southeast
Prosperity, inventiveness, and creativity reside in this corner of any space. The traditional colors to emphasize these goals are dark blue and green, along with wooden decorations as before with the Eastern segment. When you really want your muse to flower, sow a blossoming plant in a wooden container in this region. In particular, flowers with blue or yellow petals or the lotus stand out as being good choices. If your folks don't allow plants,

don't worry—just find an image of a suitable flower and put it in the Southeast instead. Remember—symbolically speaking, in a sacred space, the two are no different.

If you enjoy any type of artistic pastime and find that you're facing a block, make sure this region is free of clutter. Consider working on your current project somewhere nearby. Light both a green and blue candle while you work, adding an incantation like:

> *"Green so that creativity grows,*
> *Blue so, like water, inventiveness flows,*
> *To my eyes and spirit impart,*
> *Refreshed vision for my art."*

Take a deep breath, focus, and see what wonders arise! And make sure to save some of the melted wax. You can put small pieces in a power pouch or with your art tools to keep that creativity moving along in a positive direction.

When you're working more specifically on monetary matters or profusion in any area of your life, I suggest using more green hues in this region than blue. Green is generative and represents slow, steady growth and progress. If you're utilizing incantations, you can adapt the previous one fairly easily:

> *"Green so prosperity grows,*
> *Green abundance, my spell now sows,*
> *In my life and spirit, all wants give way,*
> *To renewed bounty—it begins today."*

For a portable prosperity charm, make the imprint of a coin in some of the melted wax before it cools and keep it in your wallet.

South

This is a region that affects many teens heavily because it governs how other people see you, whether you are accepted and respected for who you are, and your sense of power. The strongest colors to support these energies are vibrant red and purple, and the Element is Fire. Thus, you might want to decorate this region with a red or purple candle, some type of incense burner, or some other safe fire source. If you can't have any literal fire due to house rules or safety issues, look to lamps with colored bulbs or LED lights, as these all have similar symbolic value.

Just as in Neo-Wicca, the South has strong connections with the power of light. When light shines on an area, it reveals everything—both good and bad. So, whatever is located in this part of your room is very important. Make sure the images and items there are life-affirming, upbeat, and generally full of the kind of energy that you'd like other people to see in your life. For example, if you want your teachers and peers to recognize the artistic abilities you developed in the Southeast, put your best piece of work here (a way of putting your best foot forward).

One spell that you can try or adapt for this purpose begins by gazing into a bowl of water. Whisper this incantation into the surface as you watch your reflection. Envision yourself as you want others to see you and say something like:

> *"From you to me, from me to you,*
> *Begin to see what's right and true.*
> *From today to the past, from the past to today,*
> *Images of the past fade away.*
> *Look and see, look and see,*

*All I am and all I shall be.
By my will, this spell is free."*

Take the water outside and sprinkle it around you clockwise to disperse your wishes to the four winds.

One word of caution: in considering spells or rituals in this area, be aware that you're putting yourself in the spotlight. You may want attention, but the question is, what kind of attention? If you don't specify your goals here in reasonable detail, you could just as easily end up with people seeing all your faults as opposed to your attributes, especially if the spell or ritual goes awry.

To my thinking, the best application for the Southern quarter's energies is in banishing any worn-out images or expectations you have of yourself, or those that other people just can't shake. Use incense or oil infusers to accent this goal. Aromatics like sage (for wise insights), rose (for intuitiveness), and peach (for truth) are all good choices. Keep a mirror nearby while you're working so that you can look at yourself honestly, then reflect that best image to the world. As you look in the mirror, gently brush the smoke from the incense into your aura, saying:

*"Mirror, mirror, let me see,
All I am and all I can be.
Mirror, mirror, the past has no hold,
My heart and spirit are strong and bold.
Mirror, mirror, three by three,
By my will, this spell is free."*

Southwest

This region rules over relationships (especially romantic ones) and your overall happiness in life. The colors for accenting positive relationships and joy are brown and yellow, and the Element here is Earth. After all, in both life and relationships it's important to have strong foundations.

Make sure this part of your room (and if possible, the whole house) isn't blocked off in any way. Blockages keep love and joy from entering your life. If you find everyone's been miserable and relationships are constantly hitting a brick wall, check this region carefully. If it isn't blocked off physically, is it blocked from light or air? If so, bring in a lamp with a full-spectrum light bulb to bless the region. To accent this effort even more, dab the light bulb with a love or happiness oil like rose or apple, respectively. If you wish, recite an incantation like:

*"As this light shines,
Happiness and love I welcome—be mine!"*

By the way, whenever you make a new friend, a new baby comes into the house, or you get a new pet, return to this area of your room or home and enact a mini-ritual to welcome that person or animal into your life. In the next chapter, you'll find more information on creating sacred space. In this case, you'll want to call the Guardians in a manner that reflects your goals. Here's one example that you can adapt and personalize:

*"Watchtower of the East,
Let your winds wrap gently around,
To protect, guide, and give joy.*

*Watchtower of the South,
Let your fires burn gently,
Providing light, guidance, and hope.*

*Watchtower of the West,
Let your waves flow,
With healing, nurturing, and kindness.*

*Watchtower of the North,
Let your soils be sure,
Providing steady growth and foundations.
So be it!"*

You'll also need a brown candle carved with the recipient's name and a small token handy to give the friend, baby, or animal. Make sure this is appropriate to the recipient (for example, a good token for an animal might be an ID collar). Once you've created sacred space, light the candle, and ask for Spirit's blessing on the token using words like:

*"Spirit, thank you for bringing ____ into my life.
I wish to honor this new relationship with this
small token.
Bless it now with the Power of the Elements.
Bind the magic of peace, health, and joy within,
In perfect love and perfect trust,
For the greatest good.
So mote it be."*

Fill in the blank with the name of the recipient. If you're giving this to a person, you may wish to enclose a little card sharing its symbolic value. That will give it even more meaning and make it into a real treasure in the days and years to come.

West

The West rules over children's luck and future fortunes. Since you likely don't have kids yet, these energies can easily be applied to figurative "babies" —like special causes you support, your arts or sports, hobbies, or even your pets. It may also apply to children younger than yourself over whom you have a lot of influence, like a sibling, cousin, or someone you babysit regularly. The empowering colors here are white, silver, and gold, and the Elemental association is metal.

To support any one of the aforementioned areas of your life, place an item that represents the literal or figurative child in this region. Surround it with candles or other items of the appropriate colors. Each time you want to give a little more energy to that "child," light the candles and let them burn for a while as you focus your thoughts and energies. When you're finished, you can either leave the token in that region (which continues to bless it) or carry it close to your heart as a charm.

Some people claim that placing your bed here improves sleep and prophetic dreams (specifically about those literal or figurative children we're talking about). If you'd like to encourage those kinds of dreams, keep a sachet of jasmine, marigold, and rose petals under your pillow. As you lie down to go to sleep, quietly chant something like:

> *"Between the sheets and pillow seams,*
> *I will have a night filled with dreams,*
> *Each image remembered, nothing concealed,*
> *And upon waking—the meaning revealed."*

Side note: organic rose petals and marigold petals are edible and make a great pre-sleep tea. Add just a bit of sugar or honey, stir clockwise, and wish for sweet dreams!

Northwest

The Northwest region of a room or home governs helpful people in your life, like parents and teachers. It also symbolizes matters of service and networking. The traditional colors are white, silver, and gold, and the Element is metal.

The next time you're called upon to lead a school or community effort, build up energy in this area beforehand so that you can really shine (or, as the saying goes, give service with a smile and mean it). In this case, I would suggest meditating or praying here for even a few minutes every day before you begin your assigned task. Visualize yourself being very confident and successful and the effort going off without a hitch. Don't stop this daily exercise after the project begins, however. Return to this spot for a spiritual "vitamin" that will keep you going and keep your mood at its best.

If you find you're having trouble either finding or accepting help on this project (or in any part of your life), take a good look at this region. Is it blocked, dark, or cluttered? If yes, clean it up and realize that asking for help doesn't reflect badly on you at all. If anything, it shows you know your limits and respect other people's talents too. Another way to motivate yourself past that shy or embarrassed point is keeping a plain white candle in this region. Light it when you need help and leave it burning while you talk to that person. Remember, chi can't do all the work for you! Just be careful that you have a good, fire-safe container that cannot be knocked over. Extinguish the candle once you've found assistance, and remember to thank Spirit for the extra help.

This is an excellent part of a room or home in which to have a family or ancestral altar. This is where you honor and remember the helpful people in your family, those who walked the path before you. Place pictures of the people who have influenced your life the most, or those of your family line, and light candles on birthdays, the anniversary of a death, or any time you're thinking fondly of that person.

Quick Guide to the Elements

Throughout this section, you've been reading about the Elements as they associate with and accentuate a specific point on the compass. If you're having trouble thinking of what to use to symbolize those Elements, here's a quick guide that will help.

Earth
Stoneware or porcelain knickknacks (like vases or bowls), stone statues, drawings or photos of mountains, hills, forests, trees, and other greenery, hanging or potted plants, a globe, a picture of Earth from space, or your global history book from school.

Feng shui practitioners associate this Element with the conscious mind, and specifically with patience, justice, truthfulness, and order. Too much Earth in your environment and you'll tend to think too long and too hard about everything or become overly demanding. Logic becomes your ruler rather than a guide. Wood is a good balance for this type of problem.

Wood
Plants with woody stems (like bamboo), any wooden items (chopsticks, a log, a wood carving, tables, bookshelves, and even a package of notebook paper—paper is a wood by-product).

The wood Element is associated with prosperity, well-being, creativity, and family matters. Too much wood typically means you have fleeting streaks of financial fortune that quickly dwindle, or family members that constantly visit but never leave. It can also create an unyielding personality. Too little wood, however, leads to being a wallflower (unsocial) or to being irresponsible with your family relationships, money, and your health. Earth is an Element that provides balance.

Metal
Metal chimes, cookware (not stoneware, however, which would be Earth), metallic computer parts, telephones (not plastic), staples, silverware, jewelry, a three-ring binder (with metal rings), and paper clips. Whenever possible, the metal items should have rounded corners for the best distribution of chi.

Because metal was often used in currency, too much metal in your environment could lead to a greedy or exceedingly frugal nature. You might also find that you treasure magical trinkets more than the learning process. Consider balancing with a little Water, so you learn to go with the flow!

Water
Faucets, fountains, aquariums, a glass of water (or any liquid), images of oceans, rivers, waterfalls, or water-related life. Water represents power and life. It also symbolizes travel, communication, and the arts. Too much of it, however, and you could find yourself feeling limp with no sense of your own backbone and no ability to fight negative trends. Balance Water with either a little Fire or Earth.

Fire

Represent Fire with any red or orange objects—a microwave, lamps, incense burners (which can also be Air), power switches, and paintings of the Sun.

Fire offers energy, enthusiasm, warmth, joy, and light. Too much Fire leads to burning yourself out because you want to achieve too much too soon. It may also manifest as a fiery temper. Balance Fire with Water.

Color Your World

We've already reviewed some of the color correspondences for the feng shui circle, but there are more you can consider. As mentioned before, these colors and their alternative correspondences (as based in this Eastern system) give you more options from which to choose when you're designing your own spells, rituals, and decorating schemes with which to color your world with magic!

- **Black:** Black represents knowing what you should (or should not) do, try, or pursue, recognizing your attributes and limitations honestly, cause and effect, and very personal transitions. Use this color in the center of a room for best results.
- **Blue:** Blue represents improved self-image, balancing diverse factors (like spirituality and mundane life), courtesy and consideration (yours or that of another person), prosperity, and sharing. Use this color in the Northern part of a room or home for best results.
- **Gold:** In the East, this color resonates with the dragon, which represents safety, power, longevity, and wisdom. Gold is also the color of health and healing (yourself or others). Use this hue in Southern areas for best results.

- **Green:** When you have a tough choice to make, green is a very helpful color, as it encourages movement and helps overcome indecisiveness. To bring about the best choice, this color also motivates organization, logic, enthusiasm, and diligence. It is best utilized in the Eastern part of a room or home.
- **Indigo:** Indigo embodies honesty, integrity, and spirituality. It also represents our family, our ancestors, and important customs that we keep to honor both. A third correspondence is that of divinatory energy, especially for predicting the future. For best results, use this in the Northeast region.
- **Orange:** Orange speaks to us of times passage and cycles. This color vibrates with successful energy, especially when trying to overcome bad habits, fear, or other obstacles. Additionally, it can be used to motivate safety, understanding, kindness, and reliability. Orange works best in the Southeast portion of a room or home.
- **Purple:** Purple inspires authority and leadership, especially in spiritual matters. In balance to that, however, this color supports healthy meekness, benevolence, and an ongoing relationship/communion with the Sacred Parent (the God/dess). Use purple in the Northwest region of a room or home for best results.
- **Red:** As one might expect, red vibrates with active energy, especially for happiness, social outlets, and travel (adventure). It's also the color of passion toward people, the arts, a job, or learning. Red is most effective when used in the South.
- **Pink:** Pink acts very similar to red in feng shui, but on a gentler and more subtle level. Think of this as tactful interaction, friendship, short countryside trips,

and peaceful days with those you love. Use in or near the South or Southwest.

- **Yellow:** Yellow represents those things for which we hope and wish. It's also the color of experience, intelligence, personal achievement, and conscious clarity. Yellow is most effective in the Southwest part of a room or home.
- **White:** White represents the greatest good (or the Good of All). It also symbolizes your past lives, and spiritual connection, awareness, and wisdom. White works very well in both the West and in the center of a room to represent Spirit.

How might you realistically apply these colors? How about:

- Place candles of a suitable color in the region that enables the color's chi. For example, when your peers have been inconsiderate toward you, light a blue candle, carved with their names upon it, in the Northern part of your room.
- Put up sheer curtains of a specific color so that the light shines through and disperses the energy. For example, if you feel yourself coming down with something, put some sheer gold-tone fabric over your windows (especially South-facing ones) to encourage recovery.
- Wear specific colors to "put on" whatever magical energy you need, such as wearing indigo-colored clothing when you're doing rune or tarot readings (especially in the Northeast part of your room).
- Eat foods with the right colors to support your spiritual goals, like eating carrots when you need to shift your perspectives about something of which you're afraid (best eaten just before you go into that situation).

- Cover schoolbooks with colored paper that empowers your studies. In particular, yellow paper dabbed with rosemary oil is a great choice.
- Choose spell and charm components by their color (specifically by the Eastern value of that color), like using all red components as part of a charm to put in your suitcase before a trip (red cloth, red petals, red pepper, etc.).

Don't forget that you can add other magical processes to these ideas. For example, consider meditating in the Northeast (to stress your conscious mind) before decoratively covering your schoolbooks with yellow paper (especially for those classes where you're having trouble). As always, however, please only utilize those symbolic values that make sense to you, and to whatever your goals may be.

Timing Counts (Doesn't It?)

In Chapter Four, I mentioned that some people like to choose auspicious timing for enacting magic. Choosing this timing correctly supports the overall theme of the spell, ritual, or whatever. There are similar ideas in Eastern philosophies. They, too, suggested specific times as being beneficial to similarly specific types of energy. To understand this better, just think of it as adding another leg to the "table" of will and focus, making the whole thing more stable and defined.

Direction	Element	Time
North	Water	12 a.m.–3 a.m.
Northeast	Earth	3 a.m.–6 a.m.

Direction	Element	Time
East	Wood	6 a.m.–9 a.m.
Southeast	Wood	9 a.m.–12 p.m.
South	Fire	12 p.m.–3 p.m.
Southwest	Earth	3 p.m.–6 p.m.
West	Metal	6 p.m.–9 p.m.
Northwest	Metal	9 p.m.–12 p.m.

The most powerful times for each Element and direction are those middle hours. For example, the most supportive time for Water or Northern energies is about 1:30 a.m. Since one region's energies end and another one's begin at the same time (such as Fire ending at 3 p.m. and Earth beginning just moments after that) the actual hour points represent the between times when the two energies mix and mingle. Just as the yin-yang symbol blends masculine and feminine attributes into balance, these points on the clock blend Elemental and directional energies. In this manner, feng shui reminds us of how all things are connected—even things that seem opposite!

Let's try putting this together into an example. Say you've been really upset and are having trouble sleeping. That problem corresponds to the Southwest region of a room or home. It also has connections with the Earth Element. So, you might choose to bring a blessed potted plant into the Southwest part of your room after you get home from school, around 4 p.m., and do some focused spell-crafting for a good night's sleep. Alternatively, you could wear green pajamas to bed (if your reason for being upset focuses on a decision), or perhaps pink socks to re-establish a sense of peaceful foundations.

In this last alternative, you'll notice that rather than focus on a region, I looked to physical cues for symbolic value. Feet (to me) represent my connection to Earth (keeping one foot on the ground). So, wearing meaningfully colored socks makes sense. Similarly, if I were having trouble in a social setting, I might turn to wearing red gloves in colder months as we normally meet and greet with our hands. Never forget what a great tool your body can be for magic (and you don't have to remember to take it with you!).

Just a reminder: Symbolic timing helps but it's not the be-all and end-all of magical practices. If you can't work at a specific time, don't sweat it. Just add this element to those occasions when you can do so without turning everything else upside down.

No Room at the Inn?

If you don't have a room of your own, you'll have to find creative ways of applying this chapter to whatever space you use when you want to be alone and redirect the energy in your life. For example, if you're out in the woods and decide to use a flat rock for an altar or as the center of your sacred space, consider setting up that surface or the surrounding area using feng shui guidelines (you may want to take a compass to make things easier). Or, while you're in the bathroom, take a shelf or another flat surface and arrange it with little tokens to support the positive flow of chi. As with all forms of energy manipulation, your intention, will, and focus alongside meaningfulness are the most important tools.

Expectations

What exactly can you expect from blending feng shui with magic? Mostly gentle, slow changes. No matter our age, many people live out of balance. We succumb to family and social expectations rather than staying true to one's sense of self. Even a few years of having unbalanced chi requires patience and time to repair. Additionally, long-lasting transformation is typically (and frustratingly) slow sometimes. Just like anything else, keeping good energy in your life means using old-fashioned persistence and ongoing maintenance. You won't find quick fixes here, just helpmates.

Remember that feng shui isn't just about external actions either. It's about the internal process those actions represent. Our bodies are the figurative "room" for our spirits, so the truest and best work must begin within. Get rid of the clutter in your mind and heart. Release that which you no longer need, or those things that aren't healthy. Clean up your spirit and light the candle that is your soul. As you do this, you'll naturally find that everything improves both mundanely and magically. Oh, yes—if you find you enjoy feng shui as an adjunct to your magical practices, remember to have a section for your notes on it set up in your Book of Shadows!

Chapter VIII

Rituals Around the Wheel

Ceremony and ritual are an integral part of the human experience. Be it the traditional Yule gathering, the kind of cake Mom bakes for your birthday, or the send-off you get before entering college, each of these occasions and many more speak of customs and beliefs. Each also creates the perfect environment in which to nurture people's bonds with family, friends, teachers, and peers. Perhaps equally important is the fact that rituals create a sense of continuity—they remind us of progressions within and without the community around us. They speak of our life's ever-turning wheel (which seems to move faster and faster the older you get), and everything it means to be a human being.

While it might seem like the rituals in your life don't happen very often, they're actually part of your everyday activities. Take a look at your routine. You get up at about the same time, follow the same route to the kitchen, use your favorite cups for soda or juice, walk to the bus stop by the same path, and so forth. These are very real rituals that provide your life with rhythm and pattern. Now, think of what happens when something interrupts your comfortable pattern. Doesn't the whole day somehow seem "off"? We need our rituals because they provide structure and a framework.

The main difference between what happens on a day-to-day basis and a more formalized magical ritual boils down to your intention (will) and focus. Now, rather than just following a routine out of habit, the spiritual pattern you create has power and purpose. Instead of being a bystander, you will be taking an active role in life as your own Priest or Priestess.

Before that idea puts you off, you need to know that you already act in this capacity every time you make an ethical decision. Most people your age want very much to be treated and seen as young adults. In this context, especially for personal rituals, you are just that, with all the rights and responsibilities that go along with it. Spiritually speaking, every witch's goal is to become their own sovereign and guide, second only to Spirit. Creating and taking an active role in rituals is one way of starting to do just that, but you don't have to learn it all overnight. This chapter is a good starting place but remember to take it at your own pace.

Sacred Space

Ritual isn't about just illustrating a cycle or celebrating a specific transformation; it's about fulfillment. During a ritual, you fulfill your spiritual nature, and your magic becomes the bridge between this world and the astral realm. In fact, the root word for *ritual* means "fit together" —in this case, specifically fitting together the mundane and magical, the temporal and eternal (along with various metaphysical techniques and even a wide variety of people) into a functional whole. This fitting together is so important that some ancient people felt that without certain rituals, the world itself would stop spinning, and magic would die. Here is a list of the many needs that rituals satisfy:

- Illustrate our beliefs
- Give outward form to inner transformations
- Build power that can be directed toward goals
- Connect us to other realms
- Encourage us to remember our spiritual and human role in life
- Reflect the seasons and cycles or honors other important moments, individuals, or beings
- Bring people together to celebrate their commonalities

With this importance in mind, many witches choose to work rituals within the safety of a sacred space. Think of sacred space as a sphere of energy that keeps unwanted influences out and your magic in until you're ready to send it toward your goal. Just like a sink plug holds water in place until you release it, this bubble allows you to fill a regional bubble that will be guided neatly on its way before the ritual ends.

So, how do you go about creating sacred space? Well, I'm going to show you one way here (there are many others, so consider this a generic pattern that you can consult and alter as needed). Please know, however, that your attitude is just as important as all the external actions. When you approach something respectfully and with honorable intention, that starts the process quite naturally, and if that's all you have time to do, it's a great start!

Ten Steps for Creating Sacred Space

Helpful hint: Transfer this to the ritual or sacred space section of your Book of Shadows. You can adapt this particular invocation to many different magical pursuits simply by changing the wording.

Gather together four candles: one blue, one red, one yellow, and one brown or green. Put these at the Western, Southern, Eastern, and Northern points of your work room, respectively. Also, have long-handled matches ready and, if you wish, one white candle in the center (or one that you've made) to represent Spirit.

Settle into the central part of your workspace. Breathe deeply and center your spirit, focusing your mind on your goals for this day.

Light one of the matches and walk to the eastern candle, putting the flame to the wick saying:

*"Guardians and Watchtowers of the East,
I call and charge you. Come, be welcome.
Protect this sacred space from all things under
your charge. Breathe on me with the winds
of inspiration and hope."*

Move clockwise to the southern candle. You may need to keep your hand in front of the match head so the flame doesn't go out while you're moving. As you go, visualize a line of white light connecting the two points together. Put the flame to the wick saying:

*"Guardians and Watchtowers of the South, I call
and charge you. Come, be welcome. Protect this
sacred space from all things under your charge
and ignite in me the spark of magic."*

Continue moving clockwise to the western candle. Visualize this connected to both the southern and the eastern candles by radiant light. Put the flame to the wick saying:

"Guardians and Watchtowers of the West, I call and charge you. Come, be welcome. Protect this sacred space from all things in your care. Wash over me with waves of comfort and insight."

Continue on to the northern candle, extending your visualization, and putting the flame to the wick (or, if necessary, lighting a fresh match first) saying:

"Guardians and Watchtowers of the North, I call and charge you. Come, be welcome. Protect this sacred space from all things in your dominion. Grant me rich soil in which my spirit may grow."

Finally, move back to the center, saying:

*"Great Spirit, Guides, and Ancient Ones, I welcome you to this time of study. Help me in my tasks this day _____.
So be it."*

[Fill in the blank with more details on your goals for that ritual and any other personal affairs with which you'd like Spirit's assistance.]

Light the central candle (if you've used one) and visualize the outlines of your circle now slowly expanding to create a complete sphere of protection all around, above, and below you. Continue on with the rest of the activities planned for the ritual.

When you're finished, and you've guided magic on its way, it's good to thank the powers and release them from their tasks. One example that you could use is:

> *"Powers and Guides, Watchtowers All—*
> *Thank you for hearing my spirit's call.*
> *Above, below, around, within,*
> *Here our magic now begins.*
> *And as you go upon your way,*
> *Bless all you pass with joy, I pray,*
> *And while your magic grows within my heart,*
> *We merry meet, and merry part."*

Ground yourself. Ritual takes a lot of time and energy. You may want to have a snack ready. In particular, root vegetables like carrots work wonders for helping you readjust to mundane reality. Crunchy snacks like pretzels also seem to work for me.

A prayer like this one accomplishes much. It shows appreciation for all that you have, and all that may come from the ritual. It also seeks blessings on all things that come in contact with your energy or the Powers, thereby recognizing life's web. Finally, it gently reminds you that magic is not simply about this moment—it's about every moment of every day, and that's the real ritual!

Self-Preparation

Before creating or enacting a ritual, it's very important that you're in the right frame of mind (as it is for spells, divination, and meditation). Your body and spirit also need a brief self-check. Let's start with the physical aspect since this one is often the hardest to control.

Make sure you're well-rested before you begin. If you've been cramming for exams, this is not the best time for a long ritual! Similarly, if you've been sick, stressed, or feel burned out, my best advice is to wait until your body is in good condition (aches and pains really distract your focus and willpower). One thing that I like to do is have a luxurious pre-ritual bath. I use aromatic bubbles that mirror my goals and sprinkle very fine glitter on top to create a more magical ambiance. Warning: Large glitter flakes can clog drains, so avoid those.

Here's a list of potential aromatics and the energies they bear:

- **Apple:** joy
- **Ginger:** energy
- **Jasmine:** meditative focus
- **Lilac:** peace and harmony, conscious mind
- **Lotus:** spirituality
- **Nutmeg:** psychism
- **Patchouli:** safety
- **Peppermint:** conscious mind
- **Rose:** love
- **Sage, Myrrh:** cleansing
- **Violet:** well-being

You can also use this list if you'd like to anoint your body before the ritual. Choose up to three aromatic oils that represent your goals, blend them gently together, and then dab them on to invoke the energy within you. If you wish, you can add a self-blessing to this process. For example, dab your third eye, saying, *"Bless my inner vision to see truth and beauty,"* and dab your heart, saying, *"Bless my heart that I might be able to freely give and receive love."*

In terms of mental preparation, take at least five or ten minutes before the ritual to think about what you're about to do and why you're doing it. Make those all-important self-checks regarding motivations, focus, intention, and will. If you sense that anything is "off" during this time, reconsider whether you want to enact a ritual right now. Even if the timing is ideal, your mental space is very important to the success or failure of the rite.

I also find that meditation, visualization, and deep breathing help me turn my mind away from mundane matters. If you're not overly familiar with the process of meditating, it's not that difficult. The hardest part is maintaining your focus and sitting still for more than five minutes (see the section on meditation in Chapter Three). Start by taking in a deep breath through your nose and out through your mouth. Repeat this breath, keeping the cycle connected and fluid. As you feel yourself relaxing, visualize the air as if it were filled with brilliant white light that fills every cell of your body. This visualization may make you feel warmer, tingly, or more energized—these sensations indicate you're doing it the right way!

At this point I like to say a prayer before starting the ritual. I know a lot of people are uncomfortable with the idea of praying because it reminds them of church and everything associated with that, but praying is something important for witches and Pagans, too. Prayer, just like sacredness, is about your attitude—the reverence and respect with which you wield your magic. Praying creates a bridge between you and the God/dess over which important messages can come. Prayer fulfills the spiritual portion of the body-mind-spirit triad. Once prayerful rapport is established, it takes very little to keep it going in the sacred space because you've already done all the physical and mental work—in other words, you're good to go!

What should you say when you pray? Whatever you want! This is, after all, a form of communication. Just remember to do as much listening as speaking. Here's one example of a prayer that I've said before ritual (Note: If you follow a specific God or Goddess you'll want to call on Him or Her by name and adjust your prayers to reflect your relationship with that Being):

> *"Great Spirit, I come before you in a space between moments. This is a time that is not time, where anything is possible. I open the door of my heart. Come join me in my sacred space. Guide my ritual. Speak to my spirit and bless my magic so that it works for the greatest good. Thank you for all you do, all you are, and all you will be in my life. So, mote it be."*

Take that attitude of gratitude with you as you set up the atmosphere and overall stage of your ritual.

Atmosphere and Staging

I often talk about ritual as if it were a theatrical production, and in many ways it is. At least one of the functions of ritual is to help us make the leap from the temporal to the eternal, from mundane to magical. That means that this "play's" setting and props support that goal, and they should also reflect the overall focus of the ritual.

Let's go over some basic staging and ambiance helps and hints for ritual:

- Make sure you won't be interrupted. This isn't as easy as it sounds if you're working at home and have siblings, ringing phones, or insistent pets.

- Survey the region in which you're working. Is it tidy and safe, considering all the actions called for in the ritual? If not, make any necessary adjustments. For example, if you're planning a clockwise dance to raise energy, make sure there's nothing on the floor that could trip you and that your candles won't be knocked over by your movements.
- Consider what aromatics, decorations, music, and other touches are best suited to your ritual's theme. While these sensual cues are really just helpmates, each time you add one, it tends to improve the overall results because you have a better connection to what you're doing and why. Better still, some decorations can become tools in your ritual. For example, if you're having a special birthday ritual for a friend and decorate the space with ribbons, you can place knots in the ribbons that are filled with wishes for him or her. Later, present these ribbons on top of your gift (opening the knot releases the magic). I'll review some other handy decorations under "customization" next in this chapter.
- Spiritually cleanse the space, all your tools, and any components you intend to use. Where before you made things tidy for safety, now think about the overall vibrations in this region. Sprinkling around a little lemon water, or burning some cedar are two good ways of eliminating negativity or those random "off" vibrations that don't match your goals.
- Spiritually cleanse yourself. While we touched on this in personal preparation, there's often a gap in time between when you can prepare yourself and the ritual itself. During that time, your focus and willpower can shift to other things quite easily (especially if your life is busy). So, just before you create or enter

a sacred space, take a moment to breathe deeply, release any tension, and bring your inner awareness back "online" for the task at hand.
- Finally, consider what may be the very best time for you to enact your ritual. The exact moment the figurative curtain rises on your magic can make a great deal of difference in the results you achieve. Please refer to "Timing" in Chapter Three for more ideas about when you might like to schedule your ritual to give it the greatest possible amount of cosmic support.

Customizing

As with spells, you're likely to come across many prefabricated rituals in nearly every magical book you read. And, as with spells, it's perfectly okay to customize and personalize them so they're more meaningful and focused on your vision and goals. Here are just a few ways to accomplish that:

- **Costume:** Dress up! What we wear influences how we feel. So, if you're doing a spring ritual, for example, wear light, breezy clothing that reminds you of that season and those energies. If you're doing a ritual to help yourself find the right after-school job, wear professional clothing that represents the position for which you're applying. And, if you're doing a ritual to honor a God or Goddess, dress in something suitable to that Being's culture.
- **God/dess imagery:** If you've chosen a specific deity (or several) to build relationships with in your magical path, having an image of them present during ritual makes perfect sense. A white candle can represent Spirit, but other more depictive items are even better.

Look for magazine pictures, small statues, or perhaps you're artistic enough to craft your own imagery. In any case, bringing that image into the ritual honors the deity and welcomes that energy into your working.

- **Tweaking the props:** We've already talked a little about how working a good ritual is a bit like putting on a good play with more spiritual overtones. Not all props that people recommend in books are suited to your environment or your personal path. For example, some people like to call the quarters using a sword (something I doubt your parents would appreciate unless you're in the SCA). So, you'd probably want to use a wand or even your finger instead. Look through the list of props the ritual gives you, see what you have (or what's appropriate), and then switch things out as necessitated by your focus and the rules of the house.

- **Adapting invocations, spells, and meditations:** Sometimes a ritual seems really well-constructed, but the focus is completely wrong for what you want to achieve. Other times the words of the invocations, the components of the spells, or the symbols in the meditations may seem completely wrong or unrealistic. So, change them! Take the concepts and format, pull out what doesn't work, and add something from your own heart and spirit. Remember, as always, to maintain a strong sense of continuity between the substitutions you're making and your goal. Also, take the time to read the whole thing over again when you're done. Don't just read with your eyes, read with your heart to know if it sings the song of your soul.

- **Alternative settings and timing:** Since not everyone drives and not everyone has ready access to bus or subway routes, some of the suggested settings for a prefabricated ritual might prove impossible for you. Additionally, if the hour suggested is after curfew or during school, again, it becomes impossible to accommodate that framework. So adapt! Really, any place and any time is "right" for magic so long as your heart and mind are properly focused. However, it does help if you can find a setting and a time in which you won't be interrupted and, if possible, ones that have symbolic value. For example, I frequently can't celebrate Halloween on its normal date just because of family duties. So, I might celebrate some other "New Year's" ritual (there are dozens of New Year's dates throughout global traditions) or I might hold a ritual another day at midnight (an hour that's in between one day and the next, as Celtic New Year is in between one year and the next). By making these kinds of changes, you honor the ever-turning Wheel of Time, but in a way that makes sense in your life.

Once you're done with all this customization, don't forget to transfer those really good rituals into your Book of Shadows for future use!

Rituals Beneath the Moon and Honoring the Sun

The witch's Wheel of the Year has eight major points that honor the movement of the Earth around the Sun. It also has lunar rituals that mark the changing Moon phases. I'm going to review these and lunar celebrations somewhat briefly here. Why? In part because they're covered so often in other books, but also because I feel that personal rituals are a little more important at this time in your life.

When I look at my home, I notice that we have various ways of marking the turning of the seasons already—things like spring cleaning, shopping for school clothes, decorating for Yule, and so forth. These actions are mini rituals to which you can bring a little extra meaning just by shifting your demeanor and awareness of the magic in that moment. For example, when I spring clean, I often add some specially blended oils to my wash water. Exactly what oils I use depends on the needs in our home at that moment, but no matter the choice, the magic is there, as is the mini ritual! The only difference is that I added one meaningful action and made myself aware of the ritualistic overtones of what I was doing. You can do this too! And considering how busy your life probably is, you'll find this approach to honoring the Wheel of the Year very friendly to your schedule.

So, since there's already a simple and effective way to stay in touch with the Wheel of the Year, it would seem to me that the next logical focus is on those things that really change you as a person. Ritual is all about integration and fulfillment. When something happens in your life that you want to take root in, ritual is the best way to help manifest that goal. I know that as a teenager, my life could change dramatically in the span of a few days, and without a moment to breathe and think about those changes, it got a little overwhelming. Stopping for even a brief ritual can provide a break from the pressures of home and school (which are perfectly normal but not perfectly easy to cope with).

Having said all that, let's take a moment to review the Wheel of the Year and lunar rituals so you have this information as a resource when you want to create a more formalized ritual based on these themes. You may want to include this information in your Book of Shadows, along with any ritual you create for these time frames.

Eight-Point Solar Wheel (Sabbats)

- **Candlemas, February 2:** Honors the Goddess Brigit (Ireland), who presides over creativity and handcrafts. Magically, a period of gestation (of letting seeds grow in our hearts). Banish any negativity in your life and celebrate life's possibilities. An alternative name for this holiday is *Imbolc*.
- **Spring Equinox, March 21:** Honors the Earth's rebirth and the Sun's rejuvenated light and warmth. Celebrate freedom and new beginnings today. Work magic for any new pet project to bless and empower it or focus on personal growth so those seeds you've planted begin to blossom. An alternative name for this holiday is *Ostara*.
- **Beltane, May 1:** Also called May Day, this is a time to meditate on yourself as a sexual being. You have a lot of decisions to make in this part of your life, and they should be well-considered ones. It's also an excellent time to work Earth magic.
- **Summer Solstice, June 21:** The Sun's at its highest point, so shine that light on any lingering shadows in your life. Find out the truth about a situation. Gather and bless magical herbs in the Sun's warm rays.
- **Lammas, August 1:** Lammas is the first harvest, so consider what you wish to gather into your life. It's also a celebration of Lugh, Celtic God of craftsmanship, so if you've been thinking of attempting a new art or creative endeavor, bless it in your ritual today.
- **Autumn Equinox, September 22:** The days are growing shorter now, so focus on conserving your time, energy,

and resources. Also, stop to give thanks for your blessings, both big and small.
- **Hallows, October 31:** Also called *Samhain*, this is the new year, and just like the mundane new year, get rid of old junk you no longer need in your life and welcome new changes. It is also a great time for divinatory efforts.
- **Winter Solstice, December 21:** Yule is the end of the solar year. The days will now, finally, grow longer again. The magical focus is on hope, renewal, health, and kinship.
- **Lunar Observations (Esbats):** There was a long-held notion that a witch received power from the Moon, which explains in part why lunar observations were common. Also, as an easily observed shining object in the night, the symbolic value of the Moon's phases wasn't lost on early people. Here they are for your Book of Shadows:
    o **Waxing Moon:** The Maiden/Son aspect of the Moon, slowly growing. The energy in this Moon is, likewise, upbeat and progressive. Cultivate positive characteristics and skills now and focus on productivity or opportunity.
    o **Full Moon:** The Mother/Father aspect of the Moon in its maturity. This phase supports magic for achievement, completion, self-actualization, and abundance.
    o **Waning Moon:** The Crone/Grandfather aspect of the Moon as it shrinks. Banish any negativity, reinforce your protective spells, and work magic for wisdom.
    o **Dark Moon:** A void. The time of rest. If there are any figurative weeds in your life, pull them out now.

If you'd like a whole book of rituals that includes lunar and solar examples, check out my *Witch's Book of Ceremonies and Rituals*.

Personal Rituals

It's hard in a book of this size to give you all the rituals you might need for personal observances. So, I tried to pick out the ones that I thought would be helpful to the majority of readers. All of these can be adjusted to better suit your personal vision, and all of them could be used as a template for creating your own rituals, too. Feel free to tinker! As you do, you'll discover more and more about your feelings toward various magical methods and what works best for you.

Self-Dedication
Assuming you haven't done this yet, self-dedication is the moment at which you declare your intention to follow a magical path to your higher self and the Divine. This isn't the same as an initiation (which typically is done in a public setting). Rather, it's a private moment between you and the universe where you make a promise to use what you learn for the greatest good and to devote a certain amount of time and energy to your Craft. Needless to say, this should be a well-considered moment in your magical life. Of all the rituals in this section, this is the one you should consider personalizing greatly so it's as meaningful as possible.

Personal Preparation and the Sacred Space
Before a dedication, try to take at least several hours alone to think about why you're making this step. What does magic mean to you? Why have you chosen Neo-Wicca as

your spiritual path? Trust me when I say that the "whys" of your faith are more important than the "hows."

At the end of your introspection, consider taking a ritual bath. Leave any tension and negativity in the water. When you get out of the tub, also try to leave behind any mundane thoughts. Start focusing on the magic right then and there. Get dressed in whatever special outfit you've picked out for yourself.

For the sacred space, have all your tools on the altar, one candle for Spirit, one for you, one for your path, and if possible one for each of the four quarters (color-coded—blue for Water, red or orange for Fire, green or brown for Earth, and yellow for Air). Also, bring anything else that to you represents this choice. You may also want to bring your Book of Shadows into the space so you can write about this moment in the diary portion.

Invocation

As part of learning to trust yourself, you may want to seriously consider writing your own invocation for such a personal ritual. However, here's one that you can adapt or use as a prototype. Start in the East, lighting the candle (if you placed one there), and proceed around the space clockwise lighting the other candles as you recite their Elemental invocation.

To the East/Air: "Come to me, winds of change, come with the breath of life and magic."

To the South/Fire: "Come to me, fires of transformation, come with the light of understanding and magic."

To the West/Water: "Come to me, waves of inspiration, come with the waters of creativity and magic."

To the North/Earth: "Come to me, earthen foundations, come with the rich soil of growth and magic."

To the Center: "Come, Ancient Ones. Come, God/dess. Please witness my dedication as I take my first step today on the path of magic."

Meditation/Visualization
I like to open nearly all my rituals with a meditation and visualization because it helps me separate myself from more worldly thoughts. If you find that meditation is difficult for you, try other ways of helping to shift your awareness toward magical working (such as chanting, drumming, or dancing).

I find it's easier to sit down for meditations (I get lightheaded otherwise), so make yourself comfortable. Breathe deeply and evenly. Let go of any thoughts other than those about your dedication. Close your eyes and see yourself in your mind's eye even as you sit right now. Notice how the edges of your body glow slightly. That's your aura. Focus on it and let the light continue to grow outward until it fills the area in which you're doing your magic. This not only protects you but brings more personal energy into this rite. You may notice the room feels slightly warmer or you get tingly; that means you're doing it right. Once you've got the visualization to the point where your aura is clear, vibrant, and extended, move on to other activities.

Other Activities

I usually suggest taking time to pray if you've chosen a specific God or Goddess to follow. If not, speak your intentions to the four winds and the universe. As with the invocation, direct your words to each quarter and then to the center point. Be honest and real, remembering that the commitment you're making is not only to Self, but to the Spirit in all things. Here's a sample:

To the East: "Winds, hear my words. This day I commit myself to studying the magical arts and applying their methods to my life. Bless my ears that I might hear only truth. Bless my mouth that I might speak with honor."

To the South: "Fire, hear my words. This day I commit myself to studying the magical arts and letting them live through my thoughts and deeds. Bless my eyes that they may seek out your light and my heart, so it sparks with perfect love."

To the West: "Water, hear my words. This day I commit myself to studying the magical arts and letting that energy flow to all parts of my reality. Bless my hands that they are ever ready to give and receive from what I learn."

To the North: "Earth, hear my words. This day I commit myself to studying the magical arts, and having that seed grow steadily in my mind and soul. Bless my feet that I may walk gently on the Path of Beauty wherever it takes me.

So be it."

After the dedication, this is an excellent time to cleanse and bless your magical tools if you have not done so already. For cleansing, use some type of incense smoke (like cedar) or a sprinkling of lemon water. For blessing, you can simply place your hands palm downward over each tool and ask the Divine to help you in learning to use that implement effectively.

Closing

Opening a circle brings to bear all the sacred energies. Closing one thanks them for their time, releases those energies, and provides you with a sense of completion. Here's a suitable example for this ritual:

> *"Earth, Air, Fire, Sea,*
> *Thank you for sharing this day with me.*
> *Now that magic's growing in my heart,*
> *Merry meet, and merry part.*
> *Farewell."*

If you haven't done so already, now is a good time to make notes about the way the ritual felt and anything special that happened during it in your Book of Shadows so you can look back on it again in the years ahead.

Magical Naming

After taking the step to commit yourself to the path of magic, another ritual you may wish to consider is that of choosing and declaring a magical name. Let's start by figuring out how one goes about finding just the right spiritual name. Some people are lucky. A name comes to them in a dream or meditation and they just know it's the one they want to use in sacred space. If that happens to you—fantastic! Run with it! If it doesn't happen this way for you, don't worry. There are other perfectly valid ways to find a good magical name. Here are just a few ideas:

- Look up the meanings of names in baby books. Make a list of those that best represent your spiritual goals and choose from among them. Bear in mind that no one but you need to know this name (in fact, many practitioners have more than one name—one they use in circle, and another they use in private ritual and prayer).
- Consider the names of flowers, trees, animals, or crystals that you find particularly inspiring. Review the magical energies of these natural things to be sure that the name you take brings positive vibrations into your life each time you say it.
- Look up the names of people from the culture where your personal God or Goddess figures originate (for example, if you follow Athena, it might be neat to find a Greek name).
- Look up names of people from the culture in which your path originates (for this and the point above, just be careful of appropriating cultures that you don't have a connection to).
- Think back to when you were younger—was there ever a name you gave yourself and never told anyone else about or a name you wished you'd been given? That may be your magical name!

Names are very important to us, and if you don't think so, just watch what happens when you repeatedly mispronounce someone's first or last name! Names identify us and have certain energies associated with them. So, don't rush the process of finding a magical name. The best comparison I can give you personally is that it's like your favorite food or snack. When you figuratively "eat" that name, it should taste good all the way down to your toes. When you say it out loud, it needs to make you hum inside. When you close your eyes and sing it or think it, it makes you truly happy.

I do advise avoiding cutesy-sounding names like Moonbeam Rain Bunny. Trust me when I say you'll grow out of that phase really quickly. Magic is power—it's not "cute" power, it's real and vibrant. You want a name that speaks with that kind of authority in your magic.

Personal Preparation and the Sacred Space
Once you've found your name, the next step is declaring it to the Powers and Spirit in ritual. This is an important step because it makes the name yours (kind of like reclaiming lost property—this name has always been a part of you, you're just taking it back and accepting its power). To prepare for this ritual, bring items into the sacred space that represent the best of your chosen name's meaning and characteristics. Refer back to the name books to determine meanings, as well as any books that include magical correspondences. For example, if you've chosen a name that means happiness, surround yourself with things that vibrate with that energy, like lavender flowers, marjoram herb, and amethyst crystals. In addition to this, pick out one candle to represent the "mundane" self, and another to represent your spiritual self (with the new name). Carve that name into the second candle and put both on your altar.

Invocation
Start with the mundane self-candle lit. As before this invocation starts in the east because it marks a new beginning for you. (By the way, other rituals sometimes begin in

a different quarter because the energies of that quarter accent the working more strongly).

> *To the East:* "*It's the dawn of a new day.*
> *The winds of morning reach across the horizon,*
> *To join me and witness my naming.*
> *Be welcome!*"

> *To the South:* "*The sun shines on this moment.*
> *Its rays beam down with warmth and joy,*
> *To join me and bless my naming.*
> *Be welcome!*"

> *To the West:* "*The water sprinkles*
> *gently around the sacred space,*
> *Cleansing and healing,*
> *To join me and prepare*
> *my spirit for a new name.*
> *Be welcome!*"

> *To the North:* "*The seed of magic planted*
> *in my heart opens.*
> *The earth blossoms excitedly,*
> *To join me and give foundations to my new name.*
> *Be welcome!*"

Meditation/Visualization
Get comfortable and begin to breathe deeply and evenly until, as one breath ends, the next begins effortlessly. There is no time here, no rushing, no expectations. Simply be. See yourself in your mind's eye even as you are in your sacred space at this moment. Above your head, the letters of your new name have been carved into the darkness with white, sparkling light. Look at

the beauty of it. Know what it represents to you. Reach up and take one letter at a time down and place it into your heart. When the whole name is there, whisper it to yourself nine times in sets of three. Do this slowly, feeling every letter and every vibration it puts into your mind, spirit, and body.

Other Activities
Now it's time to share your name with the four quarters and Spirit. Stand and face each direction and say something like:

> *To the East: "Air, hear my words. I have chosen a name to honor my path and my choice to practice magic. Starting today, I claim the changing winds in the name_____ for use in the sacred space."*

> *To the South: "Fire, hear my words. I have chosen a name to honor my path and my choice to practice magic. Starting today, I claim the light in the name _____ for use in the sacred space."*

> *To the West: "Waves, hear my words. I have chosen a name to honor my path and my choice to practice magic. Starting today, I claim the thirst-quenching energy in the name _____ for use in the sacred space."*

> *To the North: "Earth, hear my words. I have chosen a name to honor my path and my choice to practice magic. Starting today, I claim the rooted strength in the name _____ or use in the sacred space."*
> *To the Center: "Spirit, hear my words*

and witness this rite. I have chosen a name to honor my path and my choice to practice magic. Starting today, I claim the spiritual power in the name _____ for use in the sacred space."

Now, light the candle representing your new name from the self-candle. Leave them both to burn, as the person you are doesn't disappear just because you've taken a new name. Rather, that person will grow and change to reflect that new name.

Closing
I would suggest closing with a personal prayer that thanks the Powers for their presence, releases them, shares all the good attributes you have found in your new name, and expresses your hopes to Spirit that these characteristics be activated daily in your life. When you're finished, blow out the candles and celebrate! It's your naming day (akin to a birthday), so do something special.

Blessings
There are a lot of times when we want to ask Spirit to bear blessings on ourselves, an animal, a friend, our homes, and our magical tools or components. The purpose of this ritual is to be a "generic" blessing ritual that you can customize to suit the item, person, or space to whom the blessings are being extended.

Personal Preparation and the Sacred Space
This is going to depend a lot on what you're blessing. If you want to extend good energies to a friend or family member who cannot be present, for example, you will want to have a picture of that person on which to focus.

For pets, you want to avoid a lot of flame, which can spook them. Rather, I'd use incense (a gentle "fire" with symbolic aroma). This choice is also good when you're blessing a room or home because the smoke expands outward carrying that energy wherever it goes. When doing a self-blessing, I often suggest an aromatic oil that you can dab on your pulse points as part of the ritual.

Invocation

I strongly suggest adapting this invocation to more specifically apply to that which is being blessed. This sets up a sympathetic atmosphere in the sacred space that's aimed toward your goal from the outset. Fill in the blanks below with the name of the item, person, or animal being blessed.

To the East: [Open your arms, close your eyes, and breathe deeply.] "Welcome, Winds of blessing! Guardians of the East, stand watch over this sacred space as [I/we] call in energy to inspire and motivate positive magic for _____."

To the South: [Open your arms and keep your eyes open— South is the region associated with your eyes because of sunlight.] "Welcome, Fires of blessing! Guardians of the South, stand watch over this sacred space as [I/we] call in your power to purify and energize magic in _____."

To the West: [Put your arms down, elbows at your hips, palms outward as if to meet an ocean wave.] "Welcome, Waters of Blessing! Guardians of the West, stand watch over this sacred space as [I/we] call in energy to heal and nurture magic in _____."

To the North: [Crouch down and put your fingers on the floor—if you're outdoors actually plant them into the soil to connect with earth.] "Welcome, Earth of Blessing! Guardians of the North, stand watch over this sacred space as [I/we] call in your power to give _____ firm foundations and magical growth.
So be it."

Meditation/Visualization

This meditation/visualization is aimed at drawing down white-light energy and directing it toward the person, item, or object you're blessing. It helps to have this focus present or something that represents it that you can hold in your hands or place just beneath your palms.

Begin by getting comfortable and placing the symbolic or literal item toward which the blessing is going either in your hands or on the floor in front of you. If the object is in your hands, you can start the visualization; if it's on the ground, sit close by and hold your hands over the top with the palms down. This allows energy to go through the center of your hands, which is a very traditional means of blessing in many of the world's spiritual tradition.

Breathe deeply and begin to see a swirling white-blue light forming over your head. It twirls clockwise and shimmers with life. This light becomes a funnel that moves downward through the top of your head, through your neck, into your arms, and through your palms into the thing being blessed. You may feel warmer or slightly tingly as this happens, but try to just relax and let the flow happen. Think of yourself like a pipe, and your hands as the faucet for the energy you're directing. Slowly the swirl above you totally empties itself through your hands. The item should now appear in your mind's eye as if it's filled to overflowing with the same white-light energy. When it does, the main part of this working is completed.

Other Activities
If you follow a particular God or Goddess, this is an excellent time to pray for His or Her blessings, as Spirit is the glue that holds our magic together!

Closing
Dismiss the quarters in any way you feel suitable. The short dismissal in the first ritual, for example, can be altered slightly to reflect this ritual's focus:

> *"Earth, Fire, Water, Wind,*
> *Today the blessings will begin.*
> *Sparks, Soil, Air, and Wave,*
> *Thank you for the blessings you gave!*
> *And as to the Universe your Powers release,*
> *May the magic never cease!"*

Banishing
Magic bends and changes. Banishing specifically bends and turns negative energy, a ghost, or bad luck away from you. The purpose of a banishing ritual is to either send the unwanted energy pattern back where it came, disperse it (to dispel the power), or channel it through the earth to ground it out (which neutralizes it). All three approaches have merit, but of the three I prefer the third because once the energy is neutralized it's clean—meaning

you can turn around and use it for your spells, rituals, or any other workings!

Personal Preparation and the Sacred Space
When you're working with unproductive energy, it's particularly important that you're cleansed and protected. Take a quick shower before your ritual and then dab yourself with a warding oil, such as patchouli or violet (Note: Patchouli is rather strong, so use it sparingly unless you want everything you wear to smell like patchouli for a long time). As you rub the oil into pulse points, visualize your aura as a solid sphere with a reflective surface facing outward to reflect any negativity that may come your way during the ritual.

Invocation
I'd suggest trying to write your own invocation this time. You've read several examples in this chapter, so ask yourself what it is you're banishing and how the Guardians and Elements can best help you with that problem. Don't be shy—give it a try! You'll find that the more you think about your magic and the more personal effort you put into a ritual, the better it will work. Also, invocations don't have to rhyme or follow any particular pattern, but with banishing, it's good to start in the North (to ground out the energy) and move counterclockwise (to diminish the overall power). Remember this symbolism for other rituals where you feel you want to decrease various types of influences. Clockwise movement generates positive energy, and counterclockwise movement lessens or shrinks. This is why some witches like to dismiss the circle by moving counterclockwise—it unwinds the spiral of energy in the sacred space and provides closure.

Meditation/Visualization

In your mind's eye, try to maintain the image of your reflective aura as you work. Next, bring up a picture of the source of negativity as best you know it. If you're not sure where the problem is coming from, see it as a blob-like brackish ooze. Now, with conviction, grab hold of the source and push it down into the earth. Stomp on it. Pack it into the ground until it completely breaks apart and turns into a softer brown/black hue (like that of rich soil). You should notice a distinct shift in the overall energy around you when this happens, often as if a stifling weight has been lifted from your chest. Turn away from that place in your imagination and don't look back (you don't want to re-accept that negativity). Return to normal levels of awareness.

Other Activities

I like to light candles in every room of my home after this meditation and burn some upbeat incense to reinforce the energy shift. A blend of vanilla and rose is particularly nice, representing peace, protection, love, and health. If that's not possible, turn on a bunch of lights or open the drapes to let natural light into your room or house. You've banished the shadows, so let the sunshine!

Closing

This is one of those times when you may wish to release the circle clockwise, especially if your invocation was counterclockwise. The lessening of negativity has already been accomplished, now you want to take that neutrality and turn it in your favor by way of generating positive energy in and around your sacred space. Here's one example:

To the Earth: "*Guardian of the North, thank you for grounding out the negative energies today. Now take that mulch and create rich soil for my magic to grow in.*"

To the Water: "*Guardian of the West, thank you for washing away the dangerous tides today. Now take those drops, cleanse and purify them, then water my spirit.*"

To the South: "*Guardian of the South, thank you for burning away the darkness today. Now take those ashes, mix them with the water and earth, and create a light that shines on my soul.*"

To the East: "*Guardian of the East, thank you for blowing away the negative winds today. Now replace them with fresh winds that inspire my mind.*

Merry meet, merry part, and merry meet again. Farewell."

Final Words

What I've shared with you in this book comes from nearly forty years of exploring and practicing the Craft. Even so, please know that my way is not the only way. Each person is unique and special, and therefore their approach to magic is likewise unique and special. I hope you've found these words helpful, but if any portion isn't, don't be afraid to put my book aside and seek out another path, philosophy, or method that really motivates you to be the best human and spiritual being you can be in body, mind, and soul.

On the other hand, if you've found this helpful, then you may want to go on to read *Your Book of Shadows* (the original version of this book). *Your Book of Shadows* will give you a complete Book of Shadows with which to work and many ideas for further refining the one you've started. I wish you great success on your adventure in magic, lots of fun and laughter, and, most importantly, fulfillment.

Fair winds and sweet water be yours—now and always.

—Trish